I Christen Thee,
Nebraska

I Christen Thee, Nebraska

History of the USS Nebraska And Nebraska Related Naval Ships

Monty McCord

foreword by
Admiral Hank Chiles, USN (Ret)

iUniverse, Inc.
New York Lincoln Shanghai

I Christen Thee, Nebraska
History of the USS Nebraska And Nebraska Related Naval Ships

iUniverse books may be ordered through booksellers or by contacting:

iUniverse
2021 Pine Lake Road, Suite 100
Lincoln, NE 68512
www.iuniverse.com
1-800-Authors (1-800-288-4677)

ISBN-13: 978-0-595-36655-2 (pbk)
ISBN-13: 978-0-595-81078-9 (ebk)
ISBN-10: 0-595-36655-4 (pbk)
ISBN-10: 0-595-81078-0 (ebk)

Printed in the United States of America

For Ann

*"A good Navy is not a provocation to war.
It is the surest guaranty of peace."*

—President Theodore Roosevelt
December 2, 1902

CONTENTS

ACKNOWLEDGEMENTS

Books are seldom written without the cooperation and assistance of others. I would like to take this opportunity to offer my thanks to individuals and organizations who helped with this project.

First of all, my heartfelt thanks to Admiral Hank Chiles, USN (Ret), for taking time from his busy schedule to read the manuscript, offer suggestions and write a Foreword for this book.

Rear Admiral Melvin G. Williams, Jr., agreed to read the manuscript, offered suggestions and opened some doors, for which I'm most grateful.

Thanks to Robert Conley, Clint Orr and Jerry Swift, board members of the Big Red Sub Club (BRSC), who offered photos, news clippings and other information. Clint Orr helped immensely with mailings of historic clippings and information regarding the battleship *Nebraska* and the cruiser *Omaha*.

Melvin Millsap, Fleet Admiral, and Gloria LeDroit, Chief of Staff, of the Nebraska Admirals Association offered back issues of the organization's newsletters which helped fill in their history.

Dean R. Courtney, of the Public Affairs Department of General Dynamics Electric Boat Division was a great help in supplying much needed photographs.

Very sincere thanks go to Davis Elliott, Technical Information Specialist at the Navy Department Library, Washington, D.C., for the great information and photos of *The Mariner*; and to Wendy S. Gulley, Archivist for the Submarine Force Museum for supplying a most sought after photograph.

Thanks also to the Nebraska State Historical Society staff for providing a wonderful archive of photographs and material on the battleship *Nebraska* for me to inspect.

As always the librarians at the Hastings (NE) Public Library, in particularly, Linda Gardner and Beth Martin, were wonderful and always helpful in searching for that obscure book or article.

Thanks to my friend Jean Lukesh, a fellow author and lover of history, who led me to further information on Nebraska related ships.

My appreciation goes out to Ed Buczek, Public Affairs Officer at Naval Submarine Base, Kings Bay, for the great photos he supplied.

Thanks to Allen Beermann, Executive Director of the Nebraska Press Association and BRSC member for his time and input.

My sincere thanks to the Department of the Navy, Naval Historical Center, which has always proven to be an extremely valuable archive on ship histories and photographs.

My heartfelt admiration and appreciation is extended to all past, present and future crewmembers of the USS *Nebraska* SSBN-739, and the entire United States Navy for their professionalism and for the sacrifices they make while performing their duties.

My friend, Felicia Cogley, agreed to spend her time and expertise in proofreading the manuscript of this work, which was very helpful.

And finally, to my wife Ann, to whom this book is lovingly dedicated, thank you for your patience, support and valuable assistance, which was all so very much appreciated.

FOREWORD

For a mid-western state, Nebraska has had an unusually deep relationship with the United States Navy with a number of ships bearing the name "Nebraska" or named for well-known Nebraskans, cities, counties, rivers, or other Nebraska-associated entities. Perhaps this is not so surprising considering the number of

"Nebraska Admirals" and the flooding propensity of the Missouri, Platte and Elkhorn rivers. Monty McCord has compiled an interesting history of these ships beginning with the Civil War era even before Nebraska entered the Union as the 37th state.

Certainly, the early 20th century battleship USS *Nebraska* BB-14 (but you must read the book to truly appreciate this designation) and the nuclear ballistic missile submarine USS *Nebraska* SSBN-739, most appropriately receive the bulk of Mr. McCord's attention. They have notable similarities. Each ship was outfitted with the greatest offensive firepower of its respective eras. Neither ship fired a shot in anger in our country's wars (To date this is true for the SSBN-739; we hope it will always be so). The USS *Nebraska* BB-14 went in harm's way to perform valuable convoy escort duties but never engaged the enemy in battle at sea in World War I. By all known measures, both were and are winners. BB-14 excelled in competition with her peers in gunnery, signaling and, yes, even in football. SSBN-739 has won multiple major battle efficiency competitions, two Meritorious Unit Commendations, the Omaha Trophy (awarded to the top strategic unit in the country), multiple awards for personnel excellence and continues to set a very high standard. Both have connections to the Pacific Northwest. BB-14 was constructed there, and now it is the homeport for SSBN-739.

The deterrent role of these ships ability to project power far from American shores to dissuade a potential aggressor deserves particular mention. BB-14 sailed peacefully with the Great White Fleet of 1907–1909. The fleet was a highly mobile force, which openly demonstrated that the United States possessed a powerful, well trained, modern Navy ready and able to project power overseas. BB-14 bristled with weapons. SSBN-739 also has a principal mission of deterrence that continues today. The ship is capable of high speeds with great submerged endurance, survivable and silent on patrol, ready for action, connected to the National Command Authority, invisible in the ocean depths, or when appropriate, very visible as a symbol of national power.

It is interesting to note that the United States' submarines were not historically named for states or cities. In fact, until the 1960s most submarines in our Navy were named for fish. The pattern changed when ballistic missile submarines were named for famous people in American history. The budget battles of the late 1960s and early 70s prior to authorization of a new class of attack submarine and the Trident ballistic missile submarines led Admiral Hyman Rickover to observe, "Fish don't vote." Hence, most follow on submarines were named for cities and states.

Both ships received great support from the citizens of Nebraska. This has taken many forms from the gift of a silver service for the battleship to the wonderful outpouring of support for the SSBN. The Big Red Sub Club brings crewmembers to Nebraska towns and events and has sponsored visits for Nebraskans to the SSBN-739 in her two homeports.

It was my pleasure to accept USS *Nebraska* SSBN-739 into the fleet on commissioning in July 1993. It was a very warm welcome (in fact, stifling hot even on the waterfront in New London, Connecticut), but the many Nebraskans present were undaunted and provided a fitting celebration for the namesake of a highly patriotic and most supportive Heartland state. God bless USS *Nebraska* and all who serve on her, and God bless Nebraskans for their superb support to the crew.

Admiral Hank Chiles, USN (Ret)

A 1960 graduate of the U.S. Naval Academy, Admiral Chiles began submarine training the following year. After serving on the *Triton* SSN-586, *Tecumseh* SSBN-628, *Drum* SSN-677 and *Gurnard* SSN-662, he subsequently served as Director of the Prospective Commanding Officers Course, Commander of Submarine Squadron THREE and Commander of Naval Training Center San Diego. In 1988 he reported to Italy as Commander Submarine Group-Mediterranean. In 1990, he assumed duties as Commander Submarine Force-U.S. Atlantic Fleet. He became Deputy Commander-in-Chief and Chief of Staff, U.S. Strategic Command in 1993. The following year he assumed the position of Commander-in-Chief, U.S. Strategic Command, which he held until his retirement in 1996.

INTRODUCTION

As I stood on the dock at the Bangor submarine base waiting in great anticipation for the arrival of the USS *Nebraska*, I studied the many scenes before me. The historical significance of the event in which I was taking part, wasn't lost on me. In the distance, mountains were partially obscured by fog, and trees covered most of the surroundings of the large bay. I tried to soak in everything, the navy band readying their instruments and receiving last minute instructions, the officers, chiefs and enlisted personnel decked out in their dress blues forming into lines, the nearly endless stream of wives and mothers with babies in their arms or in strollers, the official U.S. Navy photographer making his rounds and the dock workers making final preparations. As part of a delegation of some fifty enthusiastic Nebraskans who attended the change of port ceremony to show their support for the *Nebraska*, I was in awe. I squinted into the distance once again but was interrupted by a beep-beep-beep, like a truck backing up. Except this was no truck. A *huge* yellow crane was rolling toward us. We estimated after quick speculation that the machine had to be ten stories high. Everyone moved back so the crane could proceed and park right in front of us! We realized why, when we saw the workers begin attaching the crane's cables to the all-steel brow that would serve as a bridge between the dock and the submarine. We proceeded to search the end of the bay and several minutes later noticed the sail of the *Nebraska*. Two tugboats met the sub about the time we could make out some of the crew on the bridge. The tugboats replaced the sub's propulsion system inside the harbor. They ever so slowly pushed the looming ship from starboard, sideways to the dock in front of us. The sub grew in size as it approached and we saw the familiar white numbers "739" at the bottom rear of the sail. The boat's captain, Commander Christian Haugen stood on the sail with the periscopes and the U.S. flag. Two armed sailors stood by topside as the deck crew prepared to dock. The band struck up and played "Anchors Aweigh." The wives waved small American flags and looked anxiously for a glimpse of their loved one whom they hadn't seen for the last two and a half months.

This was but one more chapter in the history of a naval ship named *Nebraska*, which actually began during the Civil War. I firmly believe the old idiom that we can't know where we're going if we don't know where we've been, so I considered it important to place the *Nebraskas* within their historical context. To see when, how and where they reside in the U.S. Navy's history is important in painting their picture.

The USS *Nebraska* battleship was launched in 1904 and was a member of President Theodore Roosevelt's Great White Fleet that circumnavigated the globe, 1907–1909. The massive USS *Nebraska* SSBN-739 nuclear Trident missile submarine, one of eighteen *Ohio* class boats, is at the forefront of deterring nuclear aggression against the United States. Included in this volume is a look at Nebraska name-related ships and a naval museum right here in Nebraska. This book is a tribute as well as a historical look at the ships. Who were the ships' builders? Where were the ships based, and what were/are their missions? The reader also will learn just what "Big Red" Pride is, and how the chant "Go Big Red" has taken on a whole new meaning.

Chapter 1

The First *Nebraska* and the pre-1900 Navy

The United States has a long history of scrambling to build a navy when war was imminent, and neglecting it between times. When our young colony yearned for independence from Britain, only a volunteer militia and no navy at all existed. When war came, an Act of the Second Continental Congress passed October 13, 1775, formed the colonial Navy. It was comprised of four privately-owned merchantmen converted to warships by the addition of sixteen inferior six-pounders and several swivel guns. Even though Admiral Alfred Mahan's classic book, *The Influence of Sea Power Upon History*, which described the need for a strategic navy, wasn't published until 1890, the colonial Americans realized the need to defend their coast from British attack and to be re-supplied by sea.

In 1783, a peace treaty was signed which confirmed independence. The new nation was busy organizing a new government and gave little thought to the Navy. Most were of the opinion that it actually contributed little to the victory and if it weren't for help from the French navy, the war would have lasted even longer. So, there was little interest in further development of the Navy. Compared to the relatively inexpensive Army, the Navy required not only personnel, but upkeep of the ships.

A new Congress was formed in 1789, and the beloved General George Washington became the first president of the United States. One of the first problems Washington had to address was the Barbary pirates. Based in the North African coast states of Tunis, Algiers, Tripoli and Morocco, the pirates captured American merchant ships, their crew and cargo as they traversed the Mediterranean Sea. The crews either were killed or held for ransom, the ships and cargo sold.

The British Royal Navy no longer provided protection, so the responsibility fell to the new nation. Upon Washington's insistence, Congress passed an act in 1794 ordering the construction of six frigates and the president signed commissions for six captains of the 'new' Navy. A stop and go method of constructing these ships and others was the result of a signed treaty in 1796 with Algiers, the worst of the Barbary States. The construction continued again because of a conflict with France.

By the time Thomas Jefferson became president in 1800, a treaty had been signed with France and the young nation stood with a formidable Navy of fifty ships. Unfortunately Jefferson's party made it clear before and after his election that the Navy would be drastically reduced in size. After his inauguration on March 4, 1801, his party began downsizing the Navy. All but thirteen ships were sold and those remaining were mothballed. Most of the personnel were discharged. After the poor showing during the Revolutionary War, the Navy had become respectable only to be dismantled at its new peak.

Pride in the U.S. Navy was renewed through the heroic service of Captain Edward Preble and the ships and crews who were sent to the Mediterranean station when the ugly heads of the Barbary Coast surfaced once again.[1]

The first few years of the nineteenth century found Great Britain engaged in an all-out war with Napoleon's France. The Royal Navy felt it was right to stop merchantmen on the high seas and take sailors against their will for impressments on their ships. This included the Americans who they still considered British subjects. Incidents grew to include impressments of crewmembers from U.S. warships. The first of these occurred in 1798 with the U.S. sloop of war *Baltimore,* commanded by Isaac Phillips. When Phillips reported the outrage to Washington he was summarily dismissed from the Navy. All commanders were instructed, "It is the positive command of the President to resist to the utmost of your power, and to surrender your ship before you surrender your crew."[2] A year later, the British warship *Surprise* confronted the U.S. Navy converted-merchantman *Ganges* with the same intent of impressments of all 'British' subjects aboard. The U.S. commander, Thomas Tingey beat to quarters (same as today's call to battle stations) at which time the British ship chose not to pursue the matter further.

The Jefferson administration continuing the anti-Navy course decided that a fleet of gunboats, fifty to seventy feet in length, would be more effective than the larger frigates, even though experience gained during the Revolutionary War with this type of boat proved them unsatisfactory. About 50 gunboats were built by 1806, each commanded by a lieutenant. These little boats were not safe at sea but the crews were expected to cross the Atlantic Ocean to serve their shifts at the Mediterranean station!

The insult of impressments by the British resulted in hundreds of men being forced into the service of the Royal Navy. Britain's war with France continued with the U.S. trying to remain neutral. When French ships docked at American ports, British warships were a common site outside the harbors. Their purpose was to blockade enemy ships from further action. This was the case in 1807 at Lynhaven Roads just inside Chesapeake Bay. Two French warships had anchored at Norfolk because of a storm and a British blockading force stationed itself outside the bay to wait for them. From this area, U.S. Navy ships went to sea en route to their Mediterranean station. Because the foreign bases needed supplies regularly, every warship sent there was heavily loaded with supplies, so much so, even the guns were inaccessible. The U.S. 36-gun frigate *Chesapeake*, under command of Captain James Barron, prepared to sail to the Mediterranean to deliver a large load of supplies and to take up patrol there. Leaving the bay, the British 50-gun frigate HMS *Leopard* hove up anchor and set sail. Barron thought nothing of it and expected the *Leopard* to head north to its base in Halifax. The British ship didn't set a northerly course, but an easterly one, ahead of the *Chesapeake* where it proceeded for several hours. Once clear away from the United States coast, she came up on Barron's frigate and advised him they had a message to deliver. Barron approved the message being delivered and welcomed a British lieutenant aboard. During a private meeting, the lieutenant gave Barron a written order from his captain that he muster his crew and allow them to be inspected and interrogated in a search for wanted British subjects. Captain Barron gave his regrets that he could not permit an inspection of his crew by a foreign nation under any circumstances. The lieutenant returned to his ship. The U.S. crew then noticed the *Leopard* had come close aboard with gun-ports open. Barron knew his guns were inaccessible, and now so did the British captain. He gave the orders to go to quarters, without drums so as to not alert the aggressors. The British captain yelled over that he had orders to remove deserters from Barron's ship. No reply was offered. The *Leopard* fired a shot across the bow of the *Chesapeake*, which was a shocking insult. Barron had sails set and started to pull away, the crew still trying to clear supplies from the guns so they could be usable but it was too late. The *Leopard* opened up with a full broadside, tearing the *Chesapeake* to bits. Wood fragments became deadly shrapnel, tearing into several crewmembers. Most reports indicate that after a devastating seven broadsides were fired, the U.S. frigate had managed to fire one cannon. With dead and wounded men covering the deck, the same British lieutenant, with a party of marines boarded and conducted a search for deserters. They removed four men from the *Chesapeake* and then set sail back to Chesapeake Bay returning to their station. The crippled frigate limped back into port the following morning, and saw the *Leopard* lying at anchor as if nothing had happened.

The citizens and naval personnel at Norfolk were outraged and this outrage spread across the states. Jefferson didn't know what to do amidst the cries for war. He attempted embargoes which weren't popular and finally issued a prohibition of any aggressive naval vessels entering U.S. ports. Aggressors were identified as both England and France. Sadly, Captain Barron was court-martialed and given five years' suspension from naval service. He did not attempt to reapply until 1818.[3]

Many more incidents occurred before war was declared against Britain in June 1812. Even though the U.S. Navy was small it experienced many successes. One was the engagement of the USS *Constitution* against the HMS *Guerriere*, a captured French frigate. The long-barreled guns of the *Constitution* decimated the British ship, making it the first of its size to surrender to an American. It was so utterly damaged that it was not worth being taken as a prize. The American sailors set fire to the *Guerriere's* powder magazine sending it to the bottom in a million pieces.

There would be many more victories as the pride of the U.S. Navy swelled, even though it had less than fifty ships at the beginning of the War of 1812 compared to Britain's fleet which was one thousand strong. Never sailing the whole fleet together prevented the British from destroying the Navy in one fell swoop. Individual or small group engagements, was the strategy which prevailed. Before the war ended, authorization was given by Congress on March 9, 1814, to build the first steam-powered warship. Robert Fulton, who had developed a steam-powered ship as early as 1807, got the job. Completed too late to see action, he named it *Demologos*, though the official Navy list showed it as *Fulton the First*.[4] She was destroyed when her powder magazine exploded in 1829, never seeing battle action.

The period between the 1812 war and the Civil War was one of new ship designs and equipment but the growth or development of the Navy as a whole was almost nonexistent. John Ericsson, a Swedish army engineer who immigrated to the U.S., tried to convince the Royal Navy of the advantages of the screw propeller to no avail, so he brought his design to America. The U.S. steam warship *Princeton* was the first to be built with the new screw type propeller.

The Mexican War of 1846–1848 did nothing to further develop our Navy because Mexico had no warships to engage. Relations with Great Britain continued to be strained however and the U.S. government finally realized the need for the Navy to effectively protect the country as well as interests abroad. Congress passed an act on April 6, 1854, which approved the construction of "six first-class steam frigates, to be provided with screw propellers and armed and equipped for service."[5] Later twelve steam sloops were ordered, "which ships shall combine the heaviest armament and greatest speed compatible with their character and tonnage." Congress held discussions during 1856 and advocated that war had been impending because we did not have an adequate Navy and furthermore as a result of building these ships, war was avoided.

The state of the Navy could not prevent the Civil War that began in 1861 however. At the beginning of the war, the home squadron consisted of twelve ships, compared with five, only ten years earlier. The entire fleet numbered only about ninety vessels of all types. Just over half of these were still sailing ships, the rest newer steamers. Early in the year Congress had approved, after urging by the Secretary of the Navy, the construction of seven sloops of war.

The new Confederacy immediately seized revenue cutters and coast survey vessels within its reach, and placed them in command of the new southern navy. Still, a Jeffersonian attitude regarding navy affairs infected the south as well which became obvious when naval officers and marines were sent to serve the army in Virginia.

The northern Navy soon blockaded southern ports greatly hampering cotton exports and importation of war materials. This success renewed the southern attitudes on the need for naval forces. Warships protected above the water line with iron plating had been experimented with in Europe before the war. By 1862, the south as well as the north began construction of the "ironclad" type warship. Of course the most famous was the single revolving turret USS *Monitor* (designed by John Ericsson) and the *Merrimack* (captured by the South and converted to ironclad CSS *Virginia)*. On March 8, 1862, the *Virginia* headed for Hampton Roads and a showdown with the Union Navy. What took place was not a showdown, but a stunning victory that made every wooden warship obsolete. The Confederate ship sunk the sailing sloop *Cumberland*, burned the frigate *Congress,* severely damaged the frigate *Minnesota*, and other smaller vessels. The next morning when the *Virginia* returned to Hampton Roads to attack again, the *Monitor* engaged her in a point-blank battle that ended in a draw. The guns of the ships could not penetrate each other's armor.

After the showdown at Hampton Roads, the U.S. Navy ordered several more monitors of different types. Some were modified versions of the single-turret design, and some were larger ships featuring double turrets.

In this history of the USS *Nebraska*, it is appropriate to include the first *Nebraskas*. At the beginning of the Civil War in 1861, President Abraham Lincoln, General Winfield Scott and Secretary of the Navy Gideon Welles devised the "Anaconda Plan," which was a naval blockade along the south and east coasts, as well as using the Mississippi River to divide the Confederacy. Secretary Welles was aided in the river plan by James B. Eads, a St. Louis shipyard owner. Eads proposed basing Union operations at Cairo, Illinois and converting boats owned by his company to river gunboats. Lack of funds and troops prompted Eads to pass along the proposal to General McClellan, the Army's commander in the west. This plan became Army directed with Navy expertise in ships, naval armament and tactics. Privately owned riverboats purchased for the force were converted to river ironclads. One such riverboat, the *Nebraska*, was acquired. As stated in *Union River Ironclad 1861–65* by Angus Konstam, *"She was acquired for the War Department in September 1862, and briefly served as the support ship Nebraska."* This means that a *Nebraska* served militarily, making it the first with the name. A short time later it was converted to an ironclad and the name was changed to *Choctaw.*

The *Official Records of the Union and Confederate Navies in the War of the Rebellion* began publication in the 1890s under the direction of the Secretary of the Navy. Contained in these records are significant passages pertaining to the first *Nebraskas.*

The first mention was in an October 12, 1861 order of CMDR A. H. Kilty to LT S. L. Phelps regarding the shipping of men on the Ohio River:

> "…and on their arrival be immediately transferred to the squadron at Cairo or to the receiving ship Nebraska, here (St. Louis)."

The *Nebraska* had not been purchased by the War Department at that time and was operating under contract. The next record was a March 17, 1862 telegram from MAJ-GEN Halleck to BRIG-GEN Strong regarding the transportation of cannon:

> "Steamer Nebraska will join Commodore Foote's expedition, the siege guns to be used in reducing the enemy's works."

In an April 3, 1862 telegram from Asst. Secretary of War P. H. Watson to CMDR W. D. Porter, instruction was given to purchase the ship:

> "You are authorized to purchase the steamer Nebraska for $12,000 and proceed immediately to convert her into a gunboat, as proposed in your letter of the 28th day of March."

A June 5, 1862 report from CMDR W. D. Porter to CAPT C. H. Davis regarding progress on vessels at St. Louis read in part:

> *"I feel certain that the three gunboats, Essex, Fort Henry, and Choctaw (Nebraska), when completed, can not be excelled by anything now built, and you will find them well adapted for the river service."*

Rapid completion of the ships was crucial as the war heated up. Problems with the cost of conversion was evident in an October 14, 1862 report from CDMR David Porter to Navy Secretary Welles:

> *"...they (Fort Henry and Choctaw) can be finished in a month and will require $50,000 each to do it. The original appropriation has run out."*

A report on December 18, 1862 indicated that the *Choctaw* was still being converted. A January 1, 1863 report of CAPT Pennock to Acting RADM David Porter advised:

> *"I am informed by Capt. Badger that the Mississippi is rising rapidly and that Choctaw and Lafayette will be sent down here according to your orders, although unfinished."*

Although not listed in a description of the *Choctaw*, it was apparently fitted with a revolving gun carriage as shown by this February 10, 1863 telegram from LTCDR Badger to Ordnance Bureau Chief, CAPT John A. Dahlgren:

> *"We require a truck carriage for the 100-pounder on the Choctaw instead of the pivot carriage...the turret of this vessel is arranged with a turntable on the center; the gun recoils on the table when it is revolved to the port it is desirable to fire from."*

Patience was running thin regarding the conversion (by the Army Quartermaster-General) of the *Choctaw* as shown by these instructions from Acting RADM David Porter to CAPT Pennock of the Cairo (IL) station dated March 4, 1863:

> *"I see we have to look out for ourselves in naval matters; the army will give us no credit. I send you a letter for Capt. Phelps. Send him up to St. Louis whenever you can, and let him get that Choctaw out of the hands of the Israelites. If she has steam and guns, and casemates plated, let us have her here. I must have something to make up for the loss of the Indianola. I want the ram power, and don't care about*

the iron. I intend to take half of it off as soon as I get hold
of her."

RADM Porter must have stirred up a bit of a fuss as only two days later this message was sent from the Quartermaster General's Office in Washington to Secretary of War Stanton (that included a description of the *Choctaw*) The message apparently wasn't totally accurate regarding the status of the *Choctaw* however:

> *"The Choctaw has already been completed, turned over to*
> *the Navy, and is now probably at Vicksburg, having left St.*
> *Louis some time since to report to Rear Admiral Porter. This*
> *vessel, I am informed, is the most powerful gunboat in our*
> *service on the Western waters, being ironclad and armed*
> *with 2 Parrott, 1–100 pounder rifles, 2 9-inch Dahlgrens,*
> *2 24-pounders, and with heavy platforms amidships for two*
> *12-inch mortars. She is also fitted with a beak to be used as a*
> *ram, and her speed is estimated at 10 miles per hour."*

A March 21, 1863 telegram from S. L. Phelps to LT Maning in St. Louis reveals the true status:

> *"Launch the Choctaw. Get the turret guns in and the two*
> *light Parrot guns aft. Finish iron on turret and pilot house*
> *as quickly as possible. Get the vessel ready to go down river*
> *latter part of next week."*

Finally on April 30, 1863 the *Choctaw* engages the enemy at Haynes Bluff, Mississippi in a diversionary attack. On May 1, 1863 LTCDR Breese sent a report to RADM Porter which stated in part:

> *"The Choctaw was struck 53 times; no great damage, but*
> *much cut up, and nobody hurt… "*

Further examination of these records indicate that a *second* Civil War era naval river steamer carried the name *Nebraska*. In LT Robert Getty's report on June 14, 1863 (near Eunice, AR) he stated:

> *"…about which time the fleet hove into sight, and when most*
> *of them had passed, one of the number, the Nebraska, when*
> *opposite Eunice, was fired into by the guerillas…I immedi-*
> *ately got underway, stood over and commenced shelling the*

town and woods on that side of the river…after which I
landed at the town and burned the entire place."

LTCDR Ramsey, Commander of the *Choctaw* (which was the converted river steamer/support ship *Nebraska*) in a report to Mississippi River Squadron Commander David Porter on November 20, 1863, mentions the second *Nebraska*:

"I got underway and convoyed the steamers Nebraska and
White Cloud by the place where the battery had been and
sent them down the river under convoy of the Signal."

Only a few days later, November 24, a report from LTCDR James A. Greer to Porter stated that near Rodney, MS:

"…they (rebels) fired upon the St. Louis and Nebraska with
musketry doing no damage."

The first *Nebraska* (*Choctaw*) went on to serve until the end of the war. A May 22, 1865 order from Navy Secretary Welles to RADM S. P. Lee read:

"You will lay up the ironclads Choctaw and Lafayette in
ordinary at New Orleans, turning them over to Acting Rear
Admiral Thatcher, when stripped and the officers and crews
are detached."[8]

U. S. Ship Choctaw off Vicksburg

The riverboat and Navy support ship Nebraska after its conversion to the ironclad USS Choctaw. (U.S. Naval Historical Center)

During 1863, the largest class of ocean-going double-turreted monitors was laid down. Called the *Kalamazoo* Class, it consisted of four huge monitors, the *Kalamazoo* (builder-Brooklyn Navy Yard), the *Passaconaway* (builder-Portsmouth Navy Yard), the *Quinsigamond* (builder-Boston Navy Yard) and the *Shakamaxon*, later named *Nebraska* (builder-Philadelphia Navy Yard). Each was listed at 345 feet 5 inches in length, displacing 5,660 tons, (the famous original USS *Monitor* was 179 feet long at only 987 tons), had two screws powered by two, two-cylinder horizontal direct-acting engines, eight boilers, and was designed to do 10 knots. Each of the two armored turrets was equipped with two-15" smoothbore guns. The *Shakamaxon's* hull was designed by Benjamin F. Delano and the machinery by John Baird. Atlantic Works of East Boston, Massachusetts was paid $322,700 for turrets and extras. Reese, Graff & Duell of Pittsburgh were paid $52,118.01 for deck plates. Total cost of the monitor *Shackamaxon* was $1,300,417.72, a healthy sum in the 1860s.

The war ended before the ships were finished however and construction was suspended Nov.17, 1865. The *Shakamaxon* was the furthest along with armor and machinery installed. They remained on the blocks awaiting the decision to complete the ships and on June 15, 1869, *Shackamaxon* was renamed *Hecla*. Two months later, on August 10, it was renamed *Nebraska*. (This was the third ship with the name). They languished six more years which allowed their wood to rot. The *Nebraska* was broken up in 1874 and the others subsequently met the same fate.[7]

The Kalamazoo class Nebraska would have been very similar, but 95 feet longer and 2,365 tons heavier displacement than the 250 foot double-turreted monitor USS Monadnock *shown here in 1864.* (U.S. Naval Historical Center)

This sadly, once again was the country's attitude toward its Navy in post war America. The Navy's remaining monitors were badly worn and many were scrapped without plans for replacement. The thinking of the day was to let the Europeans do the experimenting for us as naval vessels were quickly changing (which was true). When Congress allowed building of new steel battleships they realized that the United States had no facilities at all to roll the plating or for the forging of new guns. Flawed ship plans were purchased from Britain. The results of these plans were expensive modifications to make the new ships seaworthy. By the mid-1880s however, Secretary of the Navy William C. Whitney (who purchased the British ship plans) had accumulated the funds to contract with John Roach for the building of the dispatch boat *Dolphin* and the 3,000 ton steel cruisers *Atlanta, Boston,* and *Chicago,* which were known as the "ABCDs." These funds also paid for mills able to make the steel plating for the hulls. The new steel Navy was under construction. Under Whitney's direction, Congress approved two heavy armored cruisers (later classified as second class battleships), the USS

Maine, and USS *Texas,* displacing more than 6,000 tons each, and both capable of seventeen knots.

By 1898, U.S. relations with Spain were at the breaking point. Rebels in Cuba and in the Philippines were fighting for independence from Spain. America was appalled by the brutal treatment of the rebels. In Cuba, the Spanish authorities set up concentration camps where thousands died of starvation, sickness and torture. The United States tried to purchase Cuba but Spain wouldn't consider it. Tensions rose to the point that the American consul in Havana asked Washington to have a warship within easy reach of the island in case of emergency. Even though not yet requested, President McKinley gave the order to have the USS *Maine* proceed. She arrived on January 25, 1898, to a peaceful welcome. The battleship spent an uneventful three weeks moored in Havana harbor. Then tragedy struck. In the late evening hours of February 15, a huge explosion blew the ship out of the water, killing three-fourths of the crew. McKinley ordered an inquiry into the explosion in the midst of angry calls for war. Chants such as, "Remember the Maine, To Hell with Spain!" were common. (It is the general belief the explosion originated from an internal source.)[8] He realized the conflict could not be avoided and asked Congress for fifty million dollars "to get ready for war." The construction of several new warships was ordered, but once again, *with war at our doorstep,* our Navy had not been kept at full strength. There was no way the newly ordered ships would be finished before the end of the Spanish-American War. To meet more immediate needs, congress gave the Navy permission to buy warships from Brazil, Great Britain and other countries. Assistant Secretary of the Navy, Theodore Roosevelt excelled in enlarging the Navy. He was a recognized naval authority and had always realized the need of maintaining a strong Navy. He devoured books on naval thinking. In fact, his book, *The Naval War of 1812,* was published in 1882 and was considered an authoritative work. A fleet of privately owned smaller vessels were pressed into service as well and served as auxiliaries and gunboats. This was the state of the Navy at the outbreak of war with Spain.

The defeat of the Spanish resulted in the acquisition of new territories for which the United States would be responsible. These new territories would greatly affect future naval planning.

Chapter 2

Moran Brothers Build the Battleship *Nebraska*

Imagine leaving your family at age seventeen, and traveling alone from the east to the west coast in 1875. When you arrive in Seattle, Washington Territory, you have ten cents to your name, no friends and no prospects. Now imagine only thirteen years have passed and you own a business and hold the position of mayor of Seattle. Then at age 49, you sell your very successful shipbuilding business and build a five-story, fifty-four room mansion on your 7,800-acre island property. In a nutshell, this is the rags-to-riches story of Robert Moran.

Moran was born January 26, 1857, in New York City. His father was of Irish descent, and served as an engineer on a Union warship during the Civil War. His mother was Scottish, "the grandest mother of ten that ever lived," as he described her.[1] Robert became an apprentice machinist instead of working with his father who made sewing machine belts. When he arrived in Seattle, he had to eat on credit. He landed various jobs on steamers that carried freight and mail from Seattle to Bellingham. During his time aboard the ships he became friends with John Muir, the famous naturalist. Robert was joined later by older brothers Edward and Peter. He married Melissa Paul in 1881, and paid for transportation of his mother, five younger brothers and two sisters to Seattle. The whole family lived together at that point. Shortly after the family arrived, Robert started a marine repair business with his brothers. Their shipbuilding careers began with the purchase of a damaged steamboat which they rebuilt in a short time and resold. Customers were impressed with their quick and high-quality work. The business continued to prosper and Robert Moran was elected mayor of Seattle in 1888. The very next year, his efficiency in the new office was tested when a fire broke out and destroyed thirty blocks of the town including the Moran Brothers repair shop. They immediately rebuilt at a different location and became the Moran Brothers Company, with Robert holding the positions of president, secretary and treasurer. Peter Moran served as vice-president, Frank was foundry foreman, and Sherman was assistant superintendent of wood working, with Edward having no official title. By 1893, their new shipyard consisted of 26 acres, and equipped with a marine railway that pulled steamships out of the water for repair. They received their first U.S. Government contracts in 1895, one for a steam plant for the Charleston Navy Yard, and another for a naval torpedo boat. Moran worked hard in Washington to make sure the Navy knew his company and did some research on his competition's shipyards. He soon landed a contract for a U.S. Revenue Cutter Service (later named the U.S. Coast Guard) boarding boat. Offices were built at the Moran shipyard for naval inspectors who were required to evaluate the construction process.

Gold was discovered in Alaska in 1897, giving the company another boost in business. They continued to rebuild boats as well as construct much needed river steamers for the newly created trade routes to the north. Within six months, Moran Brothers built fourteen 175-foot, stern wheel steamers and four river barges. This amazing ship-building feat was accomplished by the company's 2,100 employees. The company's most notable project was yet to come, however.

On March 3, 1899, Congress passed an act which stated,

> "...the President is hereby authorized to have constructed by contract three seagoing coast line battle ships, carrying the heaviest armor and most powerful ordnance for vessels of their class upon a trial displacement of about thirteen thousand five hundred tons, to be sheathed and coppered, and to have the highest practicable speed and great radius of action, and to cost, exclusive of armor and armament, not exceeding three million six hundred thousand dollars each;...not more than two of the sea going battle ships herein provided for shall be built in one yard or by one contracting party;...one of the aforesaid seagoing battle ships,...shall be built on or near the coast of the Pacific Ocean..."

These vessels were the beginning of the new *Virginia* class battleship.

In the latter half of 1900, the Secretary of the Navy advertised for bids on the battleships that Congress had authorized. After receiving the bids, it was found that all of them exceeded the amount allotted by Congress. The Navy notified the bidders that they would all be rejected unless the bids were reduced to meet the appropriated funds. Robert Moran, who was in Washington D.C. at the time, found out that his bid would have to be lowered by $300,000. Knowing how important is was for the little known town of Seattle to get one of the contracts, he immediately wired the Seattle Chamber of Commerce asking them to raise $100,000 from businessmen and individuals, and his company would contribute the other $200,000, in order to secure the contract. In only three days, the citizens of Seattle raised the amount requested. The *Seattle Times* management donated $3,000, and the *Post-Intelligencer* editor-in-chief, Erastus Brainerd threw in $300. The Seattle Hardware Company offered $2,000. The largest single donation came from John Leary who gave $5,000. These were but a few of the donations received.

A contract was also let for construction of an armored cruiser (a warship with less armor and fitted with smaller guns than a battleship) to be named *Nebraska* which would be built by William Cramp & Co. of Philadelphia. Moran Brothers Company was awarded a contract to build one of the three new battleships which would be the *Pennsylvania*. Congressional members from the state of Pennsylvania, wanting their state namesake ship to be built locally, convinced the Navy to switch the names however, so the cruiser *Pennsylvania* would be the one built in Philadelphia. Moran Brothers would then build the *Nebraska*.[2] The first three *Virginia* class battleships would be the *Virginia*, *Nebraska* and *Georgia*. An explanation of how the *Nebraska* was named is included here because some materials list the *Nebraska* as, "Renamed the *Nebraska*," or "Originally named *Pennsylvania*," or, "ex-*Pennsylvania*," which is misleading to the reader. She had the name *Nebraska* before one rivet was driven into its keel. The ship never had any other name.

As far back as the Revolutionary War, ships of the Navy had been named after states. A formal policy of ship naming didn't come into use until 1819 when Congress directed that they would be named by the Secretary of the Navy under the direction of the President. First class ships would be named after states of the union, those of the second class after rivers, and those of the third class after cities and towns. This policy went through changes over the years due to the debate over what exactly was the definition of a ship of the first class, second class and so on. By 1898, all of the new steel battleships and monitors would have state names. For the first half of the twentieth century in fact, only battleships held the names of states but in 1969, the guided-missile frigate DLGN-36 was named *California*. Later, our nuclear missile submarines were named for states.

In Nebraska, a headline of the June 30, 1902, edition of the *Omaha Daily News* read, "WILL BE A FIGHTING MACHINE OF THE MOST IMPROVED KIND." It stated, "Nebraska will be represented by a fighting machine of the latest design." The article went on to fill in the public on the ship's specifications and explained that it was larger than the battleship *Maine*.

The July 4, 1902, headline in the *Omaha Daily News* read, "KEEL OF NEBRASKA TO BE LAID TODAY, Ceremonies Will Take Place at Seattle This Morning in Presence of Big Crowd.". Twenty-three Nebraska state officials including Governor Ezra P. Savage traveled to Seattle to take part in the momentous event. Savage was known as the last governor to wear a cowboy hat and project a western air in the statehouse. At ten o'clock on the morning of the fourth, a naval escort, complete with a detachment of marines and a Navy band, lead the Nebraskans from their hotel to the Moran Brothers shipyard. Even though it was a soggy, rainy Seattle day, the huge crowd cheered Governor Savage and Washington Governor Henry G. McBride as the group arrived at the yard. Over twenty naval officers and their families occupied part of the reviewing stand from which the speeches were made. Above the band was a banner that read, "Equality Before the Law," which is the Nebraska state motto. An estimated 7,000 people attended and squeezed inside a shed built for the battleship project. The shed, 930 feet long and 100 feet wide, was large enough to house the finished hull. (Ships are not actually completed at launching, only the hull fitted with all machinery in place.) After the invocation was given by a chaplain from the battleship *Wisconsin*, Governor McBride gave his welcome. Governor Savage then expressed his appreciation and explained the deep pride that the state of Nebraska had for the project. A large crane, bearing the seals of the states of Washington and Nebraska and the word NEBRASKA lit up in electric lights, lowered a section of the keel through folded flags as the band played. The two governors drove the first rivets into the huge keel and each received a check from Robert Moran for three cents, which was the going rate for such work at the time. Governor Savage "promptly declared a strike for higher wages, warmly seconded by Washington's governor and they put on their coats," the *Hastings* (Neb) *Tribune* of July 11, 1902 stated. Upon reflection, one might wonder just how humorously Moran actually viewed the comment since he *had been* experiencing labor problems. Moran's youngest son Malcolm then presented Nebraska's governor with a souvenir, the first piece of steel punched from the keel.

After the ceremony, the Nebraska delegation was given a tour of Seattle and then honored with dinner aboard the USS *Oregon*. The following day, the entourage toured the Bremerton Navy Yard. It headed south to Los Angeles and on the way home attended a concert of the Mormon Tabernacle Choir.

A little over two years later, the completed hull was ready for the official launching. Christening/launching ceremonies actually date back to the ancient Greeks and Romans. The first woman to sponsor (christen) a U.S. Navy ship was in 1846, although the British Royal Navy didn't allow women the honor until much later. The ceremony consists of the sponsor naming the vessel (*Nebraska*), saying a few words and breaking a bottle of wine across the bow. The battleship wouldn't be given the "U.S.S." (United States Ship) designation until the Navy accepted and commissioned her.

Another group of Nebraskans made the trip to Seattle, this time with a new Governor, John H. Mickey, and his daughter, Mary, who would christen the ship. She wore a narrow armband with, "U.S.S. NEBRASKA" printed on it.[3] On October 7, 1904, a gray and foggy day, it was reported that some 40,000 people packed into the Moran Brothers shipyards. Another 15,000 were watching the ceremonies from various boats on Elliott Bay. Several bands played including the U.S. Marine Band from the Bremerton Navy Yard and the U.S. Army Band from Fort Lawton. Among the pieces performed was a new "Nebraska March" which was specially composed by Professor Sol. Asher. Members of the Navy and Army sat in the reviewing stand with the Washington and Nebraska state representatives. The smaller launching stand was positioned directly in front of the ship's bow which loomed far above. More than a dozen steps lead to the elevated platform which was decorated with bunting, flags and a seal of the United States. The *Omaha Daily Bee* reported that the Seattle citizens made a holiday of the occasion, "All banks and other houses were closed from noon until 3:30 p. m. that everybody might have the opportunity to attend what is here looked on business as one of the most important events in the history of the city." Mayor Balling, of Seattle, made the opening remarks and told how important the occasion was to his city, as well as to the state of Nebraska and the nation. Governor Mickey pointed out during his address that Nebraskans didn't know much about ships but were pretty familiar with the prairie schooners that traversed the state on their way to Washington. President John Schram of the Seattle Chamber of Commerce then made a special presentation of a check to Robert Moran, for $100,000, the amount promised to help secure the bid for the ship.

Moran Bros. Company

Seattle, Washington

OCTOBER 7, 1904

LAUNCHING OF THE

UNITED STATES BATTLESHIP

"NEBRASKA"

PROGRAMME

12:30 P. M.
Gates Open to the Public.

12:30 P. M. to 1:00 P. M.
MUSIC.

Wagner's First Regiment Band

U. S. Marine Band, Navy Yard

Meier's Band

U. S. Army Band, Fort Lawton

LUEBEN'S BAND

The musical program will include the new "Nebraska March"
specially composed by Prof. Sol. Asher.

Launching program issued by Moran Bros. Shipbuilding Co. for the battleship Nebraska. (Nebraska State Historical Society)

The launch was scheduled for 2:13 p.m., as the tide would then be at its highest. Eleven minutes prior to that time, during a speech by U.S. Rep. William E. Humphrey of Seattle, a loud crash of breaking planks was heard. The *Nebraska* shook, then started down the ways toward Puget Sound. The ship's sponsor, Ms. Mary Nain Mickey, instantly grasping the situation, swung the champagne bottle declaring, "I christen thee *Nebraska!*" and broke it across the bow. Apparently the shipyard workers were overly anxious with their pre-launch preparations. Ms.

Mickey's words were lost by those not on the launching stand however, as the moment it started to move, cheers rang out from the crowds and the monitor *Wyoming* fired its guns in salute. The *Nebraska* slid into the water and glided a short distance to waiting tugs that secured the floating hull to No. 3 buoy. Back in Lincoln, Nebraska, the Burlington Railroad had organized the sounding of whistles, bells and gongs across the city at launching time at 4:13 p.m. (Central Time) which continued for two minutes.

An early 1900s postcard showing the Moran Bros. shipyard at Seattle.
Ship with three stacks in background is the battleship Nebraska.
(Author's collection)

It would take another two years to finish the ship. The Moran Brothers were frustrated by labor disputes and the many change orders that came from the Navy Department. Due to international advancements in naval warfare and shipbuilding, personnel changes in the Navy Department itself, and labor problems at Moran Brothers, the *Nebraska* took longer to build than any of the other *Virginia* class battleships. Congress had passed an act on June 7, 1900, that authorized building the final two ships of the class, the USS *New Jersey* and USS *Rhode Island*. Both of these ships were commissioned almost a year before *Nebraska*.

Common to battleships of this era, was the mounting of a fancy bow ornament in the tradition of the old figureheads. (Some ships, such as Admiral Dewey's *Olympia* featured a stern ornament as well). In order to save money, the Moran Brothers used a copy of the bow piece that was fitted to the *Virginia*, as this letter from the Navy Department to the Nebraska State Historical Society, dated October 23, 1909, explains:

> *"The figurehead or bow ornament of the battleship Nebraska is of cast iron and is a duplicate in design and finish of the bow ornament fitted on the battleship Virginia; the castings, for economical reasons having been purchased by the Moran Brothers Company of Seattle, Washington, the contractor for the Nebraska, from the Newport News Shipbuilding and Dry Dock Company of Newport News, Va., the contractor for the Virginia."*

The bow piece was probably in two or three sections, the two sides were an ornamental scrollwork and featured the federal eagle symbol as a centerpiece.

The cast iron bow ornament on the battleship Nebraska weighed approximately 4,000 pounds, and was identical in design to that which was used on the Virginia. (Author's collection)

Nebraska was finally finished after five years at a total construction cost of $6,832,796.96, quite a sum in 1908. Her final cost ran $300,000 to $400,000 more than the other *Virginias*. The battleship was 441 feet 3 inches long, with a beam of 76 feet 3 inches. Displacing 14,865 tons, almost 24 feet of the hull rode below the water. It was powered by Moran engines and Babcock and Wilcox boilers. She had a speed of 19 knots with 19,000 shaft horsepower. The *Virginia* class battleships featured double-story (superposed) turrets for the main guns. A pair of 8-inch guns was surmounted over a pair of 12-inch guns both fore and aft. This design was dropped after this class because of problems with the ship rolling in high seas due to the extra weight being mounted too high. Also, all four guns in each of the main turrets had to be aimed in the same direction. The blast from the 12-inch guns was often disconcerting to the 8-inch crew directly above. Turrets equipped with a pair of 8-inch guns were mounted one on either side of the ship. A variety of smaller guns included twelve 6-inch, twelve 3-inch, and two 1-pounder guns along with two .30cal. Gatling Guns, and four .30cal. Colt machine guns. Only the *Virginia* was equipped with the as designed four submerged 21-inch torpedo tubes when commissioned. The existing torpedoes were obsolete, so they weren't installed on the others until new models were developed. The other battleships would be outfitted a few years later.[4] The designed crew complement was 40 officers and 772 enlisted men.

During July 1906, the *Nebraska* underwent sea trials near Vashon Island on Puget Sound, which were required by the Navy to sort out any machinery problems and to test the ship's speed. The battleship reached 19.5 knots, which passed the Navy's requirements. The only notable problem occurred when one of the officers gave the order to let two anchors go while at full speed. Robert Moran, along to observe the trials, objected to the order telling them they shouldn't anchor the ship while at speed. The noise of the huge chains running out caused some degree of panic by the crew who thought a boiler had exploded. The two anchors caught on an underwater obstruction snapping both chains. Later, the anchor chains were replaced, and Moran saved the remnants to use as ornamental fencing at the entrance to his island mansion.

ship "Nebraska"   Keel laid July 4th 02,
s. Co, Seattle, Wash.   accepted by U. S. Government July 18th (

*Before a newly built ship is accepted by the Navy, it must complete sea
trials. Here the Nebraska exceeds the 19 knot minimum speed required.*
(Author's collection)

The August 4, 1906, issue of *Scientific American* magazine included a photo of
the *Nebraska* on the cover and an article explaining the ship's features. It espoused
the merits of its guns, armor and power plants and the fact that it was built, "in
the young state of Washington."

Finally the *Nebraska* was ready for commissioning which took place after
the Moran Brothers turned the finished ship over to the commandant of the
naval district. On July 1, 1907, at the Bremerton Naval Yard, the ceremony was
attended by a full marine guard, a band and officers and the partial crew complement. Before speeches are made, the basic commissioning ceremony takes place
when the district officer reads the orders for the delivery of the ship, and orders
the prospective commanding officer to "Commission the USS (*Nebraska*)." The
first commander of the *Nebraska*, Captain Reginald Fairfax Nicholson, repeated
the order to his executive officer, Lieutenant Commander Robert E. Coontz,
who relayed the order. (Coontz served as an equipment inspector at the Moran
Brothers shipyard on the battleship *Nebraska* project before being assigned to
the ship.) The bugler sounded attention and the national anthem began as the

ensign and commission pennant were hoisted simultaneously. Captain Nicholson read his orders from the Navy Department and stated, "I assume command of the United States Ship *Nebraska*." His first orders to Commander Coontz were to "set the watch," which meant the officers and crew were to man their duty stations throughout the ship. With the "official" portion of the ceremony completed, speeches were made by the Navy brass and special guests. The *Nebraska* didn't have a full crew yet, and as Commander Coontz explained, "We started to coal the ship the morning after she was commissioned, having only the musicians in the band to do the work." [5] This must have greatly dismayed the musicians who normally would be on deck playing as the coaling was underway. This was arguably the filthiest job in the Navy and always required a complete cleaning of the ship when it was finished.

Captain Reginald Fairfax Nicholson-first commanding officer of the USS Nebraska. (U.S. Naval Historical Center)

The July 4, 1908 issue of the *Omaha World Herald* reported that one George Baker was the first Omahan to report aboard the USS *Nebraska* but it was unclear whether this also meant he was the first Nebraskan. (In fact, USN vessels were and are currently manned by sailors from a variety of states). The local Navy recruiter stated that any man re-enlisting could request to be assigned to the battleship, after first attending a training station.

Interestingly, this would be the second vessel built by the Moran Brothers Co. that Nicholson would command. The first, when he held the rank of lieutenant, was the USS *Rowan* (Torpedo Boat No. 8), commissioned in 1899. Nicholson was born on December 15, 1851 and first served in the Navy as an orderly under his father, Somerville Nicholson, on the USS *State of Georgia* during the Civil War. He graduated from the U.S. Naval Academy in 1873 and was the Navigation Officer on the USS *Oregon* during her epic journey from San Francisco, through the Straits of Magellan, to rendezvous with the fleet at Santiago, Cuba during the Spanish-American War. After retirement, he was recalled into naval service to head up missions to Chile, Peru and Ecuador during World War I. Rear Admiral Reginald F. Nicholson retired a final time in 1918. He died on December 19, 1937, at the age of 86.

In 1905, then Governor Mickey convinced the legislature to authorize $3,000 for a custom made silver service for the battleship. The governor approved a contract with A. F. Smith & Company of Omaha. The service was designed for Smith by J. E. Caldwell and Company of Philadelphia and was made by Thomas G. Brown, a New York City silversmith. It consisted of a punch bowl, ladle, tray, centerpiece with candelabra, flower vase and 18 drinking cups. The four-gallon punch bowl weighed 25 pounds and had, "Presented to the U.S.S. Nebraska by the State of Nebraska 1906," engraved on one side with a Union Pacific train and a stagecoach. Above the lettering was the Department of the Navy seal. The reverse side featured the state seal above scenes of the USS *Nebraska*, a sod house and covered wagon. Buffalo and other animals are featured in the designs of the set along with a Native American, sea shells, sea horses, a cattle ranch, the Omaha stockyards and the Platte River. The tray was three feet long and two and a half feet wide, and had an engraved image of the ship. The centerpiece, a combined candelabra and epergne, weighed 41 pounds![6]

Governor Mickey received the set on November 3, 1905, and allowed it to be displayed in a Lincoln department store window for eight days where it attracted throngs of onlookers. It was subsequently sent back to Smith & Company for storage until the ship was completed.

Yet another delegation from the state of Nebraska traveled west, this time in 1908, to present the magnificent silver service to 'their' ship. Governor George L. Sheldon arrived with an unbelievable 113 state and military officials to meet the *Nebraska* at San Francisco. The group consisted of most of the state agency heads including the lieutenant governor, the governor's secretary, state auditor, secretary of state, agriculture secretary, two state senators, the inspector general of the Nebraska National Guard, various National Guard officers and a minister. On May 8, 1908, a ceremony was held with Governor Sheldon presenting the silver service to the officers and crew. According to Commander Coontz, the bay was choppy and the Governor became quite sick. The ship's surgeon treated him so he could proceed with his speech. Thousands of people had come to San Francisco to see the arrival of the Atlantic Fleet that coincided with the presentation.

After the battleship *Nebraska* project was completed, Robert Moran was worn out. Many years of hard work including his nearly total management of the Moran Brothers Company left him weak. After consulting with specialists in Europe, he accepted their diagnosis of "organic heart disease." He was told there was nothing they could do but recommended that he retire immediately. He bought the Cascade Lumber & Manufacturing Company located on Orcas Island where he planned to retire. He sold the Moran Brothers Company in March of 1906 to an Eastern concern. By 1911, he owned 7,800 acres on the island where he built a 54-room mansion that he named, "Rosario," after the nearby Rosario Strait. In 1921, he donated 2,998 acres, which included Mt. Constitution, to the state of Washington, and it became Moran State Park. Moran fooled his doctors however, and outlived his wife and all of his siblings. Moran had invested $1,500,000 in developing Rosario but in 1932, with no remaining family, he decided to sell out. The country was hard hit by the depression and Moran had trouble finding a buyer. He even ran an ad in the May 1933 issue of *National Geographic* magazine. In 1938, he finally sold the fully-furnished Rosario on 1,339 acres for a mere $50,000.[7] At 81 years of age, Moran built a new, smaller home on the island. The shipbuilding magnate died five years later on March 27, 1943.

Today, the Rosario is called the Rosario Resort and Spa, a three-star hotel with 127 rooms. It also features meeting and convention facilities, pools, restaurant and marina. The Rosario is owned by RockResorts, a Vail Resorts, Inc. company with headquarters in Denver, Colorado. Advertising indicates that a "Moran Museum," celebrating the history of the Rosario, is another feature of the popular resort.

VIRGINIA CLASS BATTLESHIPS

The USS *Virginia* (battleship #13) was built by the Newport News Shipbuilding of Newport News, Virginia. The keel was laid on May 21, 1902, was launched on April 5, 1904, and commissioned on May 7, 1906, with Captain Seaton Schroeder, commanding. She was decommissioned Aug. 13, 1920 and sunk by Army Air Service bombers off North Carolina Sept. 5, 1923.

The USS *Nebraska* (#14) was built by Moran Brothers Shipbuilding of Seattle, Washington. The keel was laid on July 4, 1902, was launched on October 7, 1904, and commissioned on July 1, 1907, with Captain Reginald F. Nicholson, commanding. She was decommissioned July 2, 1920 and sold for scrapping Nov. 30, 1923.

The USS *Georgia* (#15) was built by Bath Iron Works of Bath, Maine. The keel was laid on August 31, 1901, was launched on October 11, 1904, and commissioned on September 24, 1906, with Captain R. G. Davenport, commanding. She was decommissioned July 15, 1920 and sold for scrapping Nov. 1, 1923.

The USS *New Jersey* (#16) was built by Fore River Shipbuilding Company of Quincy, Massachusetts. The keel was laid April 2, 1902, was launched on Nov. 10, 1904, and commissioned May 12, 1906, with Captain W. W. Kimball, commanding. She was decommissioned Aug. 6, 1920 and sunk by Army Air Service bombers off North Carolina Sept. 5, 1923.

The USS *Rhode Island* (#17) was built by Fore River Shipbuilding Company of Quincy, Massachusetts. The keel was laid May 1, 1902, was launched on May 17, 1904, and commissioned Feb. 19, 1906, with Captain P. Garst, commanding. She was decommissioned June 30, 1920 and sold for scrapping Nov. 1, 1923.

Chapter 3

Member of Teddy's Great White Fleet

President Theodore Roosevelt recognized that a powerful naval battle fleet was of the utmost importance as a tool of international diplomacy. The United States was only just beginning to demonstrate its might as a world power when it defeated the Spanish in the 1898 war, which resulted in acquiring Guam, Puerto Rico and the Philippines. Concerned that the Japanese would seize Hawaii, the U.S. annexed the islands during the year as well. With new territories all over the Pacific Ocean, a larger navy was immediately justified. The President agreed with Alfred Mahan's view that a concentrated battle fleet superior to any other was necessary to maintain world sea power. The Russo-Japanese War, 1904–05, demonstrated the power of a concentrated fleet when the Japanese navy destroyed the Russian Pacific Fleet in February 1904. The Russian Baltic Fleet was sent east to deal with the attackers but was destroyed also. Japan's battleships also demonstrated the effectiveness of accurate long range guns.

The President wasn't alone in his stand for a great Navy. Among numerous civilian proponents was Professor F. M. Fling, head of the European History Department at the University of Nebraska who was quoted to say, "A larger American Navy would be desirable as a means of preventing war," when he spoke at the Nebraska state librarians convention in October 1908.[1] (The speech was made during the epic voyage of the Great White Fleet.)

Roosevelt knew changes had to be made in battleship planning and design. He organized the Newport Conference, where he set up a General Naval Board for this purpose, subjugating the various Navy bureaus who some declared were "separate fiefdoms." He also eliminated the old system of local squadrons, and the Navy's 26 battleships were formed into the Atlantic Fleet.

Relations with Japan were strained by the new U.S. presence in the Philippines. The Japanese were interested in expanding their territories and the Philippines would have been a natural asset. Additionally, many Japanese had immigrated to the American west coast, but reports of discrimination and school segregation in California increased the tensions. Fear that the Japanese would retaliate by attacking the coast reached Washington.

President Roosevelt saw an opportunity to accomplish several things by sending the Atlantic Fleet on a worldwide cruise. He did not announce a 'world cruise' however, only a training exercise for the organized fleet which would sail from the east to the west coast via the Straits of Magellan. He said the return course was not yet decided. First, he did not want the cruise to appear as a provocative move toward Japan, but he felt they needed to witness America's naval might firsthand. His famous quote, "Speak softly, and carry a big stick; you will go far," specifically indicated that the Navy was the "big stick."[2] He apparently expected resistance from Congress due to the expense of the cruise and true to form, neglected to inform them of it until it was too late. Congress would not approve the appropriations for the cruise but Roosevelt had funds available to get the fleet to the west coast. He was heard to say that if Congress failed to provide funding to bring them back, they could stay there. It was important to calm the fears of the Californians, but more importantly to put the battleships through their paces. The Navy needed to assure their dependability on an extended cruise, and to note problems that could be corrected in new ship designs. It would also be an excellent training mission for the crews as well. No other navy, up to that time, had mounted a world wide cruise of such a large fleet. It would go down in the annals of naval history.

At the end of November 1907, the fleet was furnished with tons of supplies at the New York Naval Yard. In addition to the Navy's colliers, arrangements were made with other countries for a continuous supply of coal for the ships throughout the cruise. This was a huge undertaking in itself, as each battleship would burn approximately 90 tons of coal per day, at 10 knots. In addition, the coal used by the destroyers, colliers and auxiliaries would make the fleet's daily use about 1,500 tons![3]

The President's orders were for the fleet to assemble at Hampton Roads, Virginia (site of the famous *Monitor-Merrimack* battle during the Civil War) which would be the send-off point of the cruise. The incredible fleet was manned by some 14,000 sailors and marines. The battleships were organized into divisions, with the newest and those in the best condition occupying the first two divisions. It was desirable to have the best entering the foreign ports first, to give a better impression. On December 16, Roosevelt received Rear Admiral Robley D.

Evans, Commander-Atlantic Fleet, aboard the presidential yacht *Mayflower*. He had sailed from Washington to review the fleet before its departure. He wished Evans the best and reminded him that the cruise was a peaceful one but, "If it turns out otherwise you realize your responsibility." Since the only real possible threat to the fleet would be the Japanese, Roosevelt wanted to be sure Evans had no doubt what was to be done.

At 10 a.m., the President gave the signal for the fleet to proceed. Admiral Evans led aboard his flagship, USS *Connecticut*. Each battleship fired salutes to Roosevelt as it passed his yacht. Once at sea they headed south for their first port of call which would be Trinidad, British West Indies, a 1,800 mile trip.

Battleships of the fleet were organized by squadrons and divisions:

FIRST SQUADRON

First Division	Second Division
USS *Connecticut*	USS *Georgia*
USS *Kansas*	USS *New Jersey*
USS *Vermont*	USS *Rhode Island*
USS *Louisiana*	USS *Virginia*

SECOND SQUADRON

Third Division	Fourth Division
USS *Minnesota*	USS *Alabama*
USS *Maine*	USS *Illinois*
USS *Missouri*	USS *Kearsarge*
USS *Ohio*	USS *Kentucky*

Admiral Robley Evans' flagship, USS Connecticut, leading the Great White Fleet during the historic round-the-world cruise. (**U.S. Naval Historical Center**)

The fleet included six torpedo boats (destroyers), USS *Hopkins, Hull, Lawrence, Stewart, Truxton, Whipple,* and the torpedo flotilla tender *Arethusa.* Support ships were the, USS *Culgoa* (store ship), *Panther* (repair ship), *Glacier* (store ship), *Yankton* (tender), and the hospital ship *Relief.*

Standard colors for battleships of the U.S. Navy had been established by 1890. During peacetime, hulls were white and superstructures were buff colored. During wartime, such as the Spanish-American War, the ships were repainted slate gray (battleship gray) to be less noticeable.[4] It is a commonly mistaken belief that the Atlantic Fleet (or Battle Fleet, as it was sometimes called) was painted white especially for the world cruise, and that every white U.S. Navy ship of the era, was a member of the famous cruise. Either during or after the historic event, the fleet became known as the "Great White Fleet," which helped to further these beliefs in later years. The moniker probably originated with the civilian correspondents on board the ships.

The battleship Nebraska in her white and buff peacetime colors. U.S. Naval vessels were permanently painted gray in 1909. (Nebraska State Historical Society)

The 16 gleaming white battleships steaming in two parallel rows surely must have been a magnificent sight. Keeping the coal burning ships looking that way, however, was a never-ending job. When the black smoke from the stacks curled down onto the ships, it turned everything black. Coaling the ships also provided a filthy black coating everywhere. The entire crew was required for this job, which consisted of filling 800-pound bags of coal and then mechanically hoisting them from the collier over to the battleship, dumping them on the deck or into the bunkers directly and doing it again until the ship was full. The ship's band played to help make the dreaded chore more tolerable. Most enlisted crewmen kept old worn uniforms just for this job. Once coaling was completed, cleaning the ship started until it was finished.

Daily life at sea was strictly regimented beginning with reveille at 5 a.m. The schedule was full of cleaning, battleship drills and in the small amount of off-duty time, taking care of uniforms and crew's quarters. President Roosevelt was adamant about the cleanliness of the crews, particularly during ports of call. The stokers who worked in the boiler rooms found cleanliness unrealistic however, and they rarely were allowed shore leave. Believably the worst job aboard ship, these men worked in 100 plus degree heat and choking coal dust. Many cases of insanity would be recorded with these men during the cruise.

Dust coated sailors on the battleship Rhode Island (Virginia class) after the coaling process. Cleaning the entire ship came next. **(U.S. Naval Historical Center)**

Recreational needs were impressively addressed. Each ship had at least one grand piano and a temporary stage for theatrical productions. The Woodford & Bill Piano Company of Green Bay, Wisconsin, published a series of advertising postcards after the cruise which pictured various battleships. On the backside, the company lauded the U.S. Navy's endorsement of their products;

"Uncle Sam's Choice, the most sincere test to which a player piano can be subjected is aboard a ship, yet the officers and sailors of over 50 U.S. & Foreign Battleships have purchased Autopianos, and unhesitatingly express their appreciation of the enjoyment derived from this wonderful instrument. During the famous cruise around the world of the American Fleet nearly every Battleship possessed an AUTOPIANO for the amusement and education of the officers & crew. That these instruments needed little or no repairing after having been exposed to every climate, is more conclusive proof of the remarkable durability of the AUTOPIANO and of its ability to give musical enjoyment and great satisfaction under any conditions. The marvelous Autopiano gives pleasure to every member of the family because all can play it."

Other items carried by the fleet included 60 phonographs and 300 sets of chess and other sporting goods. A large supply of cigars and cigarettes and 15,000 pounds of candy also were available. The ship's stores included a good variety of food and soft drinks. Meats included, beef, beef hearts, beef liver, chicken, clams, fish, hamburger steak, pork loins, mutton, pork sausage, turkey and veal, as well as an assortment of canned meats.[5]

A group of news reporters were picked who accompanied the fleet and wired their stories home. Negative reports about the ships or the cruise were not allowed and reports were reviewed and censored accordingly. President Roosevelt picked Henry Reuterdahl, a noted maritime painter, to capture the cruise on canvas. This turned out to be a bad choice however, when it was learned that Reuterdahl, working for *McClure's Magazine*, had written an article that pointed out many faults of the ships. The article was published just a month after the fleet left the United States. Those progressives in the Navy were encouraged by the article, but those of the old school who didn't favor change, looked down on it with disgust. When Reuterdahl left the fleet at Callao because of a serious family illness, the newspapers falsely reported that he had been expelled because of his negative article.

Just before Christmas 1907, the fleet reached its first foreign port. On December 23, the battleships entered the harbor of Port of Spain, and simultaneously dropped anchor.

The origin of the U.S. Navy Shore Patrol can be traced to this historic cruise of the battle fleet.[6] The patrol was organized especially to keep watch on those sailors enjoying shore leave at foreign ports and to apprehend any who became the slightest bit disorderly. It was of the utmost importance to Washington that the U.S. not be embarrassed. Port of Spain would be their first test.

Traditionally, a visiting foreign ship would give a cannon salute and one would be returned and then met with a welcome by the local political leader. Trinidad, a British possession, offered no acknowledgement at all of the fleet's arrival. The British, wanting to keep good relations with Japan, not to mention the great naval rivalry that existed between Britain and the U.S., decided to ignore the fleet. Admiral Evans led a party to shore and visited the governor-general anyway. Local vendors were ready for the visit however, with sailors paying inflated prices for their souvenirs which included monkeys and parrots. (Paying inflated prices would be a common problem throughout the cruise.) They took mountains of greenery back to the ships to decorate for Christmas and enjoyed the holiday with traditional dinners, games and a visit by Santa Claus.

Port stops included the unpopular coaling process. A startling discovery was made on the *Ohio*, when a half stick of dynamite was found in the coal while loading the ship's bunkers. While sabotage was a real possibility, it was believed the dynamite had accidentally come from the coal mine itself. Admiral Evans did order that every shovel-full was to be hand checked before it went into the furnaces. With coaling completed, the fleet set sail on the 3,000-mile trip to Rio de Janeiro, Brazil.

While en route to Rio, it was found that coal consumption was up in the fleet, but especially with the *Maine* (the second battleship by that name) and the *Alabama*. The poor performance of the latter was due to a cracked cylinder head. In fact, they both would continue to be a serious problem all the way to San Francisco. The traditional navy "crossing of the equator" ceremonies (which still is conducted today is some fashion) were held for all those who hadn't yet crossed. Adorned in wild costumes, "King Neptune", and his "Royal Household", (members of the crew) would present themselves, and gather those hapless sailors who had yet to cross the Equator. The sailor's hair was shaved and he was given a good rubbing of lampblack and then dumped into a pool of water which was erected on deck just for the occasion. Captain Seaton Schroeder, commander of the *Virginia*, and later Fourth Division Commander, referred to the event when he said, "That sort of thing was good for the ship. Every one of those novices began to think himself a horny-handed mariner, and with that self-appreciation there would be born a growing idea of making good."[7]

The arrival of the grand fleet to Rio was a complete opposite of the disgraceful snub at Trinidad. Brazilian warships met, saluted and led the fleet into a harbor full of welcoming citizens. A German cruiser was at anchor, which had been monitoring the fleet on behalf on the Kaiser. That night during celebrations in town, sailors were involved in a large brawl that resulted in cancelled shore leaves.

The Brazilians kept a good attitude and still welcomed the crews with open arms. Thousands of men subsequently were allowed leave with no further conflagrations.

The only port calls planned were to be in Rio and Callao, Peru, but the fleet caught the imagination of several South American countries that wanted the honor of a visit. The first of many requests was Buenos Aires, Argentina. As the Rio de la Plata bay was too shallow for battleships, the squadron of six torpedo boats was sent, and treated to a royal welcome.

The government of Uruguay was given an apology for skipping past Montevideo who had also prepared a large welcome celebration. As the fleet continued south into heavy seas, Argentinean warships caught up desiring a celebration at sea which was conducted.

The fleet soon entered rougher seas traversing the Straits of Magellan. Over the years, the merciless waters had claimed many ships. Halfway through the Straits the fleet stopped for coaling at Punta Arenas, Chile. Punta Arenas was a known gathering point for spies and it was reported that two Orientals were observing the ships from a cliff. Surprisingly, a British cruiser was anchored there and made a point to thoroughly inspect the American fleet. The Chilean government asked for a visit to Valparaiso, but Evans, not wanting to lose more time, appeased them with a fast speed cruise through the harbor where the ships fired batteries of salutes.

Eighteen hundred miles to the north, the fleet dropped anchor at Callao. Other than the *Maine* and *Alabama,* the ships had been relatively trouble free. The ships were met once again with celebrations of every sort to honor the Americans. Dances, dinners, sightseeing and even bullfights were orchestrated for the visitors.

On March 12, 1908, the fleet arrived at Magdalena Bay, Mexico, the regularly scheduled stop for coaling and gunnery practice. More dynamite sticks were found in the coal and prompted new worries about sabotage. The gunnery practice was part of an annual spring competition in the Navy which, obviously was to increase battle accuracy. In late March, during practice, the muzzle of a six-inch gun exploded on the *Missouri.* The *Hastings (NE) Daily Tribune* of March 30, 1908, reported that no one was injured but, "The gun was ripped open for a distance of 140 inches. More than half the gun was destroyed."

So far on the cruise, seven men had died of various illnesses. The health of Rear Admiral Evans was poor when the journey began, and with a continued worsening of rheumatic gout, had to finally relinquish command of the fleet. He was transported to the spa at Palo Robles for treatment. Rear Admiral Charles Thomas was in temporary command when the fleet arrived in San Diego, California. Huge celebrations including a parade were held in their honor. Several other cities requested a visit, so to accommodate them, Thomas split off the separate divisions of ships to stop at them. After being charged heavily-inflated prices at Santa Barbara, sailors staged a small riot, fighting and breaking windows. They willingly left the city and returned to their ships.

Nebraska (left) and Wisconsin at the Puget Sound Naval Shipyard just before joining the Great White Fleet at San Francisco. (Nebraska State Historical Society)

Until WWII the blue U.S. Navy caps featured the name of the sailor's ship. Shown is a pre-1920 cap ribbon from the battleship Nebraska. (Author's collection)

The largest celebrations were held in San Francisco however, the official end of the first leg of the world cruise. The fleet gathered several miles off the city where the battleships *Nebraska* and *Wisconsin* joined the fleet. Then they sailed into the Golden Gate where a reported one million spectators gathered all around the bay area to cheer their arrival. Even the Secretary of the Navy came west to review the fleet (which had received fresh paint during the voyage from Magdelena Bay). Ships of the Pacific fleet joined them at San Francisco where a parade and banquet were held for the Navy secretary and officers. President Roosevelt gave Fourth Division Commander, Rear Admiral Charles Sperry command of the fleet for the rest of the cruise. Officials of the railroad stated that they brought over 300,000 visitors to the city for the fleet visit. The ailing Admiral Evans rejoined sailors in San Francisco before heading for home. Evans must have been amused when he saw picture postcards being sold with his photograph on them, which included an inspiring verse;

> *"From the old Virginia strand,*
> *With Bob Evans in command,*
> *The grandest fleet that ever sailed, they say,*
> *Is coming to our coast,*
> *And we'll greet them with a toast,*
> *When Evans drops his anchor in the bay"*

Another interesting photo postcard was printed and waiting for the fleet's arrival to California. The front of the card featured the faces of nine women and was titled, "Members of the Young Ladies Reception Committee that will Welcome the Sailors to California." Under each lady's photo was her "name" and the name of a battleship in the fleet; MISS LULU SHUGAR—U.S.S. CONN, MISS MARY SWEET—U.S.S. KANSAS, MISS GERTRUDE CHARMER—U.S.S. LOUISIANA, MISS U. R. MINE—U.S.S. MINN, MISS MY OWN DARLING—U.S.S. GEORGIA, MISS NANCY LOVE—U.S.S. OHIO, MISS PURE HONEY—U.S.S. TENN, MISS CORA HARTBREAKER—U.S.S. NEW JERSEY, MISS U.R.A. DAISY—U.S.S. VIRGINIA.

Battleship Nebraska as she appeared during her voyage with the Great White Fleet. **(Author's collection)**

During the second week of May, the fleet sailed farther north to visit Seattle and Tacoma, Washington. Sailors were given live "Teddy" bear cubs as gifts in honor of the president. More celebrations were held for the heralded fleet in these cities.

Admiral Evans traveled by train across the country on his return trip to Washington. During a stop in North Platte, Nebraska, on May 12, 1908, the *Hastings (NE) Daily Republican* reported on a speech he made from the rear of the train. His not so veiled comments belied his feeling about politicians, "We will always have war so long as we have anything worth while to fight over and the more battleships and fewer statesmen we have, the longer we will have peace."

One of many souvenirs available when the fleet arrived in San Francisco.
The medal reads "Souvenir Visit of U.S. Naval Fleet to Pacific Coast-
Rear Admiral Evans-Fighting Bob-1908." (Author's collection)

In June the fleet returned to San Francisco to undergo repairs, painting, coaling and restocking of depleted supplies. The public was finally told what the crews already knew, that the cruise would continue around the world, transiting the Suez Canal to return to Hampton Roads. Almost immediately, Australia requested a visit by the fleet. Britain reluctantly approved visits to Australia and New Zealand, both British commonwealths. They still did not want to offend their Japanese allies but their fears were dispelled when Japan also requested the honor of a visit. The Chinese, upon hearing that the fleet would visit Japan, also wanted the fleet. China was friendly to the U.S., so to treat friend and foe alike, the request was approved.

Perhaps in anticipation of a need for the sailors to correspond with their families during their long absence, Congress passed an Act of May 27, 1908 which authorized, for the first time in history, post offices to be established aboard naval vessels. The Navy issued a General Order on June 17, 1908 which established the first naval post office in the fleet, aboard the battleship *Illinois*. The *Nebraska* established hers on August 20, 1908. These post offices were officially branches of the New York Post Office, but each ship had their own cancellation stamp.[8, 9, 10]

The addition of *Nebraska* and *Wisconsin* was originally meant to increase the fleet's number to 18 battleships, but they subsequently had to replace the troublesome *Maine* and *Alabama* who were ordered to drop out.

Battleships of the Fleet from San Francisco to Hampton Roads:

(Some rearranging of ships occurred but the *Nebraska* kept its place in the Second Div.)

FIRST SQUADRON

First Division	Second Division
USS *Connecticut*	USS *Georgia*
USS *Kansas*	USS *Nebraska*
USS *Minnesota*	USS *New Jersey*
USS *Vermont*	USS *Rhode Island*

SECOND SQUADRON

Third Division	Fourth Division
USS *Louisiana*	USS *Wisconsin*
USS *Virginia*	USS *Illinois*
USS *Missouri*	USS *Kearsarge*
USS *Ohio*	USS *Kentucky*

On July 7, 1908, only 15 of the battleships sailed through the Golden Gate on their way to Honolulu, Hawaii. Scarlet Fever had broken out on the *Nebraska*, so the crew had to be quarantined. The ship soon rejoined the fleet at Hawaii, only to have the disease surface again. The *Nebraska's* crew did not get shore leave until the last day in Hawaii.[11]

Admiral Sperry was a strict disciplinarian, and trained the fleet in special maneuvers which included "crossing the T," where a line of ships would cross directly in front of oncoming ships, and the "figure S", where the twin lines would curve left and right continuing in a full circle until they returned to their sailing formation. During a "figure S" maneuver when the ships were returning to their lines, the *Nebraska's* quartermaster was quoted, in a rather startled tone, "New Jersey coming alongside the starboard gangway sir!" As the *New Jersey* was returning to its spot in the formation, it struck the *Nebraska* causing some damage. The fleet had to stop while repairs were made, and then continued on to the next port. The *Nebraska's* doctor had been very apprehensive and irritable about the possibility of just such a collision as the *New Jersey* had come dangerously close before. His fears were not unfounded as Commander Coontz recalled, "…would you believe it, her prow actually smashed into the stateroom of this very same doctor."[12]

After 17 days at sea, through the worst weather they had yet encountered, the fleet arrived at Auckland, New Zealand. For this long voyage, the battleships carried extra sacks of coal on their decks which were drenched in the stormy sea. Dark streaks covered the decks and hulls, which precipitated cleaning and repainting before their arrival. Admiral Sperry ordered the S formation as they entered Auckland's harbor, all stopping and dropping anchors in unison. Sperry wanted a flawless exhibition for the British, which he got. The welcome was nothing like the one in British Trinidad. Hundreds had gathered and cheered the fleet's arrival. Sperry gave many speeches throughout the week of receptions, dinners, sightseeing and parties. A few sailors liked New Zealand so much they apparently were planning to stay, until the shore patrol escorted them back to the ships.

The fleet was met before sunrise by steamers full of people anxious to welcome the fleet to Sydney, Australia. Because of the thousands of citizens present, the wildly-decorated streets which included a five-story replica of the Statue of Liberty, the crew unanimously felt that Sydney had given them the grandest welcome so far. Special booklets were printed in honor of the American fleet's visit and were popular souvenirs with the sailors. Bands took pride in playing the Star Spangled Banner and nearly non-stop speeches and banquets kept the sailors busy.

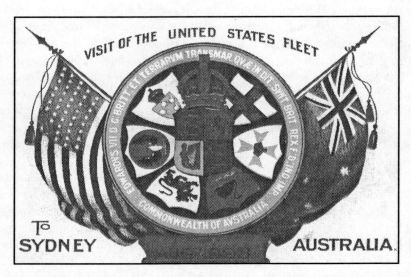

Postcard marked "August 1908" from Sydney, Australia commemorating the Fleet's visit. Hundreds of postcards were sold by vendors during the cruise. **(Author's collection)**

The city of Melbourne would be the last official stop in Australia and would top even the Sydney welcome. Unfortunately, the partying and huge crowds got out of hand. Sailors drank too much and two were killed when hit by trolley cars. Many people were hospitalized after being trampled or falling from buildings. Several sailors were court-martialed. The worst of the news was that of desertions. Some were rounded up, but it was reported that about twenty sailors failed to report, causing speculation that they stayed with their new girlfriends and future wives. Many "new" passengers appeared when they left Australia however. Dogs, kangaroos, koala bears, monkeys and wallabies found their way to the ships to join other animals picked up earlier in the cruise. The fleet made a coaling stop in Albany before heading north over 3,000 miles to Manila, Philippine Islands.

Lt. John E Lewis, USN, of the USS Connecticut, is shown with the kangaroo mascot presented to the ship by the citizens of Sydney, Australia. (**U.S. Naval Historical Center**)

The relatively new possession was a center of unrest by those Philippinos who resented U.S. rule. The minority American population looked forward to the fleet's visit which they hoped would instill some respect in a military show of force. Admiral Sperry had learned of a cholera epidemic on the islands and decided not to allow shore leave to protect his crews. The minority American population was very unhappy about his decision but Sperry was determined not to risk his crews unnecessarily.

The new battleship *Nebraska* conducted its first gunnery practice in the Philippines which was very successful. One eight-inch turret reportedly made 15 hits out of 16 shots. After the practice, the *Nebraska* became a noted ship in gunnery.

歓迎

Issued by the Department of Communications in commemoration of the Visit of the American Fleet. Oct. 1908.

***This souvenir Japanese postcard reads "Issued by the Department of Communications in Commemoration of the Visit of the American Fleet Oct. 1908."* (Author's collection)**

The fleet left the Philippines on October 10th and headed north. Admiral Sperry felt some degree of apprehension towards the next leg of the cruise, which would be to Yokohama, Japan. Many had speculated during the trip about what they thought the troublesome Japanese would do when the fleet approached. Even though their government officially invited the fleet, many feared a naval attack like that which destroyed the Russian fleet years before. A defeat of the American fleet would open the Pacific Ocean to uninhibited Japanese expansion. As they approached their destination Sperry was concerned with the news that the Imperial Japanese Navy, 160 warships, had headed south from their homeland.

The Japanese soon were replaced by the immediate concern of a huge typhoon that enveloped the fleet on the 13th. One hundred mile per hour winds and 60-foot waves played havoc in trying to keep the fleet together. The communications mast on the *Kearsarge* was toppled and several others lost lifeboats and other equipment. All ships had signs of bent railings, broken and bent masts and ladders. Sailors had been washed overboard, and all but two were rescued. The next day after the storm ended, the fleet joined again in formation, and crews commenced repairing, cleaning and painting.

When the fleet arrived in Yokohama's harbor, each of the battleships anchored next to 16 Japanese warships. The *Nebraska* anchored next to the *Idzuma*. The crews of both ships lined the decks and stared at each other as they came to a stop. Officers and sailors of the Japanese ships went aboard to present themselves as guides for the crews. Admiral Sperry received orders from President Roosevelt that only the most trusted sailors would be allowed shore leave. There were to be no disorderly sailors on this visit especially. The number of shore patrolmen was increased to help assure good conduct. The apprehension of a possible naval conflict during the visit quickly vanished. The Japanese government had spearheaded the welcoming activities. They went so far as to coach the citizens of Yokohama and Tokyo in behaviors that wouldn't offend the visitors. Vendors gave refreshments so freely the Americans didn't have to pay for most things. Vocal groups sang American songs and others treated them to free performances of geisha dances, wrestling matches and juggling acts. Rickshaw and train rides to Tokyo, 18 miles away were all free. Commander Coontz, the executive officer of the *Nebraska*, remembered three things about a dinner he attended during his visit to Tokyo, "First, as senior officer present, I had to make my first speech, second, we sat on our feet with our legs crossed under us, and third, I was able to outstare the champion starer who was a geisha girl!"[13] U.S. and Japanese flags hung from every available position. Newspapers in both countries reported the resounding success of the peaceful visit.

A rare view from the deck of the battleship Nebraska during maneuvers.
(Author's collection)

Unable to ignore the request for a visit from China, an ally, the port town of Amoy was chosen by the Navy Department because Amoy had a deeper harbor than Shanghai, and it was further away from Japan (China was Japan's enemy). The Chinese weren't happy about the choice, but agreed. Admiral Sperry decided to send only the Second Squadron to China, the First Squadron (of which the *Nebraska* was part) headed for Manila. The townspeople themselves were totally uncooperative, so the Chinese government transported tons of building materials to build a more respectable city for the fleet to visit. Called, "Pleasure City," it was basically a secured area where only special passes would allow admittance. Nearly 4,000 Chinese police and military personnel were brought in to insure security. A generating plant even had to be built as the city didn't have electricity. Before the ships arrived however, the typhoon that they had encountered at sea, hit Amoy, killing 3,000 people and destroying all that had been built. The Chinese persevered and in ten days had rebuilt the "city". Thousands of dollars were spent on entertainment of all kinds. The area around Amoy was saturated with revolutionists, who spread anti-American sentiment with threats of all kinds, and precipitated the move of more Chinese troops to the city. Pleasure City was called an amusement park without the crowds. The sailors enjoyed the food, entertainment and gifts, which were more abundantly present than the Chinese themselves. Less than 200 citizens were allowed to join the Americans in this manufactured setting, under the careful watch of armed guards. On the last day, the Chinese conducted a huge fireworks show, sparks from which unfortunately set fire to the entire Pleasure City. Local officials began accusing sailors of looting the burned buildings, at which time the crews were ordered to return to the ships. The next day, November 5, 1908, they steamed away from China. Instead of the disastrous visit, the American newspapers covered William Howard Taft's defeat of William Jennings Bryan of Nebraska for the Presidency.

The Second Division rejoined the First, who had just completed range-finder calibration exercises at Manila on November 8. Admiral Sperry learned that the cholera epidemic there was even worse than before, so again no shore leaves were granted. From November 14 through 25, the fleet conducted gunnery practice, this time replicating actual battle conditions. A 50% increase in accuracy answered the question of the crew's readiness after so many wild port visits. The people in Manila, not about to give up, sent a flood of wires to the President demanding a visit from the fleet. Roosevelt understood the risks involved, but also had to weigh the political implications. The presence of U.S. force was a necessary reminder of who controlled the Philippines. He ordered Sperry to carry out a two-day visit to Manila. The sailors went ashore and were entertained with tours of cigar factories, parades and receptions.

With coaling and final preparations made, the fleet left Manila on the morning of December 1, 1908, with homeward-bound pennants flying at their masts. They passed Singapore and headed in a northwesterly direction through the Strait of Malacca. On the night of December 8, the *New Jersey* reported two men overboard and stopped for rescue efforts. Searchlights were used but only one of the two men was found. Five days later the fleet arrived at their next port for coaling which was Colombo, Ceylon (present day Sri Lanka). The colonial government allowed shore leave for only 80 sailors per ship in the afternoons.

They were treated to dinners, receptions and concerts, and also enjoyed buying souvenirs. Many packages of tea also were brought back to the ships at the end of the day. More small animals were brought back to the ships, which by then must have made ship life a spectacle. One crewman wrote a letter home explaining that there were so many parrots they made an almost constant noise, with some learning to talk. These were apparently foul words because he stated, "A sailor's parrot would not make a good impression with 'nice' folks." He also told of a cute squirrel the chief master-at-arms had which "got tired of living for yesterday he jumped overboard."[14] Sadly, quite a few of these adopted pets would die before the cruise ended.

Baseball games were held, and the *Nebraska,* already with a champion football team (go figure), defeated the *Missouri, Kentucky* and *New Jersey* teams for the fleet championship. During the previous year, the *Nebraska's* team-members were looking for a strong catcher. They heard about just such a young man (unnamed) who lived with his uncle, a saloon owner, in Bremerton, Washington. They were able to get the uncle's permission for the boy to join the Navy and he was assigned to the *Nebraska.* During the games at Ceylon, the *Kentucky* team accused the *Nebraska* team, "…of actually buying the saloon in order to get the services of the young player…"[15]

Those confined to the battleships were entertained by a constant flow of small boats from which all sorts of items were offered for sale. The minstrel troupe from the *Georgia* came aboard the *Nebraska* to perform, which was a big hit and was part of the entertainment the ships conducted themselves.

The fleet would spend Christmas at sea, en route to their next destination which was Suez, Egypt. During this trip, incorrect signal flags went up from the *Kansas,* indicating a man overboard. The *Illinois* responded by lowering a lifeboat, during which a sailor fell and was unable to be recovered. On December 31, a signal contest was held (which apparently was needed) and the competition finally was narrowed down to the *Kentucky* and the *Nebraska.* As Commander Coontz explained, "We beat the *Kentucky* 30 hoists to 10, and felt that for a new battleship joining the fleet, the *Nebraska* had established a reputation."[16]

The fleet received a wire from Washington on New Year's Day 1909, which told of a massive earthquake and tidal wave that reportedly killed 150,000 people in Sicily. Admiral Sperry was asked what aid he could offer. It was decided to send the store ship *Culgoa* with several tons of food, and the tender *Yankton,* loaded with medical supplies and six surgeons immediately steamed ahead to Messina via the Suez Canal.

A hundred men from each battleship were given two days' leave for the opportunity to tour Cairo and the Pyramids. Resplendent in their uniforms, they swarmed the city. They quickly established a custom of trading their U.S. Navy caps for the tasseled red fezzes which were popular in that region. One can only wonder what the officers' reactions were when they saw all those red-topped sailors returning to the ships.

It took the fleet three days to transit the Suez Canal, going through in small groups. Interestingly, it cost the U.S. Navy $134,751.32 for the fleet's passage. The *Georgia* caused an additional delay when it ran aground near the Bitter Lakes, with the rest of the Second Division, *Nebraska*, *New Jersey* and *Rhode Island* stopping behind her. After a short time, she was pulled free and continued the transit. The ships continued on to Port Said for coaling. The Navy Department had to deal with rescheduling due to the Italian disaster, and a flood of visit requests from all over the Mediterranean. In order to cover the requests of Greece, Turkey and North Africa, the fleet was split up. The First Division (including Admiral Sperry's flagship *Connecticut*) went to Naples, Italy, to assist with the disaster. The Second Division (including the *Nebraska*) was sent to Marseilles, France, where they arrived on January 15. The Third Division split up to cover Greece and Turkey, and the Fourth Division did the same to visit the North African region including Malta, Tripoli and Algiers.

While at sea on the way to Marseilles, a crewman on the *Nebraska* remarked that they were hit by a sandstorm that sanded the decks, saving the crew that chore before scrubbing. At Marseilles, the crewmen were somewhat shocked by the site of horse quarters hanging in meat markets, many still with their hooves. Obviously, the horse is more revered in America than in France.

The secretary of the Navy decided to recognize the sultan of Morocco and ordered Admiral Sperry to send a flag officer and two battleships to conduct the honors. The *Georgia* and *Nebraska* arrived off Tangier on January 30. A twenty-one-gun salute was fired and only a small party of men, including Admiral Wainwright (Second Div. Commander), and the two battleship captains, Qualtrough and Nicholson, made a formal visit. Captain Qualtrough became a point of embarrassment at a ball where he appeared to be intoxicated. After he returned to the *Georgia*, he was relieved of command and later court-martialed.[17]

By the last week of January, the fleet rejoined at Gibraltar for coaling and replacement of much needed provisions that had been used for disaster relief. The fleet received an unusual reception at Gibraltar. Warships of Britain, France, Russia and the Netherlands greeted them with salutes and bands playing the American National Anthem. Surprisingly, the higher-ranking British admiral skipped the proper protocol and visited Admiral Sperry on the *Connecticut*.

On February 6, the fleet steamed west heading for the point where they began the cruise, Hampton Roads, Virginia. Final drills, inspections, cleaning and repainting were scheduled before the fleet arrived home. Days of bad Atlantic winter storms hindered the progress. Winds and high seas washed lifeboats and men overboard, constant reminders of the terrible typhoon they experienced in the China Sea. Sailors watched the ships ahead of them crest the huge waves, their sterns lifting out of the water and their huge propellers chopping at the air.

The fleet dropped anchor 15 miles off Cape Henry at 2 a.m. on February 22, the scheduled arrival day. Commander Coontz of the *Nebraska* stated, "During the darkness we slung men on stages over the side of our ship, and they painted the hull."[18] It was imperative to make a stunning appearance and all ships conducted new rounds cleaning and repainting.

A newly-formed squadron met the fleet and would escort them to Hampton Roads. The squadron included the newly-commissioned battleships *New Hampshire, Idaho* and *Mississippi*. Curiously, *Maine* was the flagship (which had been replaced on the world cruise). During the cruise, the Navy had permanently adopted the battleship gray color and the new squadron was so painted. The color, as well as the new "cage masts", made them appear quite different from Sperry's fleet.

In anticipation of the arrival of the fleet, Norfolk and other cities organized entertainment and extensive decorations easily matching or surpassing the largest displays the fleet had seen during its historic journey. Newspapers featured homecoming articles days before the arrival. The strict schedule for their arrival was necessary so President Roosevelt could receive them before leaving office on March 4. At about noon on Monday, February 22, 1909, George Washington's birthday, the combined fleets steamed into Hampton Roads to the cheers of tens of thousands of people along the shore and in small boats.[19] The gray, rainy day failed to dampen anyone's spirits however. Salutes to President Roosevelt were fired from all ships in the fleet simultaneously and then individually as they passed his yacht, the *Mayflower*. The secretary of the Navy accompanied the president, and on another Navy yacht, members of the Senate and House Naval Affairs Committee were present. After the fleet came to anchor, President Roosevelt boarded each flagship, where he spoke to the crews and officers. He told them that they were the first battle fleet to circle the globe, and those that complete the journey in the future would only follow in their footsteps.

The fleet had traveled approximately 45,000 miles in 14 months, and made 20 official port calls plus coaling stops in 26 countries on six continents. The ships consumed 435,000 tons of coal at a cost of $1,967,553. It was estimated that each ship wore out 250 shovels while scooping all that coal! They used more powder firing salutes on the cruise than was used during the entire Spanish-American War.[20]

The ramifications of the world cruise were far reaching. Not only did it prove that a large organized battle fleet could effectively circumnavigate the world (some said it couldn't be done), it demonstrated that the United States was now a world power capable of taking the fight to an enemy if necessary. It was extremely valuable as a training experience for the crews, as well as providing tested data for future battleship designs. Promotion of the U.S. Navy to the public as well as to government officials was most valuable. Future expenditures could more easily be justified with both groups. Citizens read almost daily accounts of the fleet's travels in newspapers and magazines, and in turn learned about, and became more interested in, the world around them. Many of the reporters who sailed with the fleet wrote books and magazine articles about the cruise. Many different types of souvenirs illustrating the battleships were produced for the American consumer as had been at nearly every foreign port. Picture postcards which started to become popular in the U.S. during the 1870s were the most popular item. Literally thousands had been mailed by our sailors from foreign countries to their families at home. Many were specially printed to acknowledge and welcome the fleet visits.

The cruise, unapproved by Congress, deplored by the British, feared by some as the precursor to war, predicted by many to end in failure, was one of the United States' greatest naval accomplishments which highlighted the auspicious presidency of Theodore Roosevelt.

Chapter 4

War Service & Final Harbor

With homecoming celebrations complete, the battleships steamed out of Hampton Roads to their own yards. Most of the ships were scheduled for repairs, repainting (to the permanently-adopted battleship gray) and refitting. *Nebraska* was sent to the New York Navy Yard along with *Rhode Island, Connecticut* and *Ohio,* for this work.

USS Nebraska, circa 1910, after she was refitted with cage masts and repainted battleship gray. (U.S. Naval Historical Center)

Advances of on-board equipment required the changing of the battleships' masts. Originally fitted with military masts (tubular steel poles mounted on the centerline that supported platforms for lookouts, searchlights and light guns),

they were changed to the new *cage*-type mast. Sometimes said to resemble oil der-
ricks, it was believed that these masts could sustain shell hits without toppling.
This design also was necessary to accommodate new fire-control and range-find-
ing equipment, as well as searchlights, antennas and flags. Some ships, including
Nebraska, would get only a new foremast (to which the conning tower, etc. was
attached), and receive the new cage mainmast later. By the end of 1910 however,
all ships received both new masts.[1]

The large bridges with which the battleships originally were outfitted were
changed to simple, open types, and conning towers, from which the ships were
controlled, were made larger. These changes explain the difference in appearance
of these ships when looking at old photographs.

Other changes made were the removal of the traditional bow ornaments that
so identified the battleships of this era. The *Nebraska's* ornament was removed at
the New York Navy Yard during May, 1909, and the explanation of why they were
removed was included in a November 4, 1909, letter to C. S. Paine, Secretary of
the Nebraska State Historical Society from the Navy Department;

> *"With the adoption of "slate color" as the color of paint with*
> *which to finish the exteriors of battleships, armored cruis-*
> *ers, etc., the figureheads lost their value as a feature of ship*
> *ornamentation. It was decided, therefore, to remove the*
> *figureheads from the vessels of the classes referred to in the*
> *Department's previous communication, in order to relieve*
> *the vessels of unnecessary weight."*

A favorable reply came in a July 9, 1909, letter from the Navy Department to
Congressman M. P. Kincaid (Nebraska), regarding his request that the *Nebraska's*
bow ornament (referred to as the figurehead) be sent to the state to be preserved
in the capitol or the state university museum. The letter provided these instructions;

> *"The Department takes pleasure in advising you that it has*
> *authorized the Bureau of Construction and Repair to issue*
> *suitable instructions to the Commandant of the Navy Yard,*
> *New York, to prepare for shipment to the proper state author-*
> *ity, the above noted figurehead of the Battleship Nebraska,*
> *on receipt of the address where same should be delivered.*
> *Transportation charges cannot be borne by the United States*
> *and arrangements for defraying same should therefore be*
> *made by the State authorities. In view of the provision of*
> *statute law prohibiting the actual transfer of Government*

> *property, the delivery of the figurehead in question will be*
> *regarded as a loan, subject to recall by the Navy Department*
> *if, at any time, such recall should be necessary."*

In the secretary's 1909, annual report of Nebraska State Historical Society, receipt of the bow ornament was recorded;

> *"The figurehead, or bow ornament, of the battleship*
> *Nebraska is now in possession of this Society as a perma-*
> *nent loan from the navy department at Washington, secured*
> *through the assistance of Governor Ashton C. Shallenberger*
> *and Congressman M. P. Kincaid…the figurehead weighs,*
> *when packed for shipment, 4,055 pounds. It is now in stor-*
> *age in a knocked down condition and cannot be successfully*
> *exhibited until we have more room."*

During the time the *Nebraska* spent at the New York Navy Yard, many of the ship's officers and crew were rotated out. Captain Nicholson was made Chief of the Bureau of Navigation, with Captain John T. Newton replacing him as command-ing officer. Lieutenant Commander Coontz was promoted to Commander, and even though he made 23 separate applications to attend the Naval War College, Captain Newton requested that he stay on as executive officer for another year.

In July, *Nebraska*, with other ships, steamed to the South Atlantic for training and gunnery exercises. While towing a target, a line separated and flew towards the stern where Commander Coontz had been watching. It struck him and sent him flying backwards, landing under the aft netting. Although badly bruised, it was fortunate that he wasn't knocked overboard.

By September, 1909, Coontz accepted the position of Chief of the Buildings and Grounds at the United States Naval Academy, no doubt disappointing Captain Newton.

A collision occurred in December between the *Nebraska* and sister ship, *Georgia,* while conducting drills in the South Atlantic. The December 11, 1909 edition of the *New York Herald* reported that while the *Georgia* was leaving the fir-ing line and meeting the *Nebraska* which was heading to the line, the newspaper was told the latter suddenly swerved from its course and headed for the *Georgia*. The *Nebraska* struck the *Georgia's* port side, causing some dented armor plates. Damage to the *Georgia* was a bit more extensive, "…lost a portion of her forward bridge and had two seven inch guns damaged." It was expected that she would have to be detached from the fleet and sent to the Norfolk Navy Yard for repairs. Two signalmen on the *Georgia's* bridge were thrown to the deck about 20 feet below. The extent of their injuries was not reported. The *Nebraska* was apparently under the command of Captain Hugo Osterhaus, who was to be promoted to Rear Admiral, but the collision evidently postponed the honor.

The following year *Nebraska* attended the Hudson-Fulton Celebration at New York City, and participated in a naval parade. The celebration commemorated the discovery of the Hudson River by Henry Hudson in 1609 and the first successful steam navigation of the river by Robert Fulton in 1807. The *Nebraska* also steamed to New Orleans in 1912 for the Louisiana Centennial.

Nebraska served port blockade duty at Vera Cruz, Mexico, to protect American interests during the revolution from May 1 to June 21, 1914, and again from June 1 to October 13, 1916, and earned the Mexican Service Medal. After a period of reduced service, she was placed in full commission again on April 3, 1917, and was at the Boston Navy Yard undergoing repairs when the U.S. entered World War I. Under the command of Captain Guy H. Burrage, *Nebraska* was assigned to the Third Division, Battleship Force, U.S. Atlantic Fleet, and headed for the Chesapeake Bay for training and tactical maneuvers on April 13. She continued these exercises all along the east coast until returning to the Boston Navy Yard for repairs, January–February 1918.

***Anthem Nebraska Sheet Music* (Author's Collection)**

The crew of the *Nebraska* published a piece of music called *Anthem Nebraska*, which was written by Chief Yeoman Henry L. Lee and arranged by H. D. Chittim. The cover featured the U.S. coat of arms, naval and U.S. flags, a photograph of the battleship and a statement, *"Being The Pledge Of The Crew Of An American Man-O-War To Their Ship."* Printed inside was, *"Dedicated to Captain Guy H. Burrage United States Navy."* The words were as follows:

> *Onward sail onward, on to victory,*
> *Flaunting our ensign, Pride of the sea,*
> *To you Nebraska, we pledge to thee; Our*
> *life our love allegiance and loyalty."*

The copy in the author's collection was apparently mailed by a sailor on the *Nebraska* as it is inscribed on the back cover, *"To Miss Anne Johnson Buford Ark, From J. Vance Johnson, U.S.S. Nebraska div 15, c/o Postmaster, New York City, N.Y."*

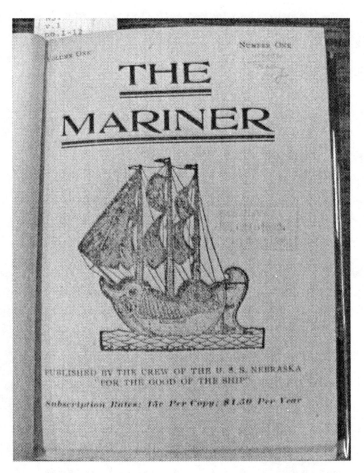

Cover of The Mariner, published by the crew of the Nebraska from Jan-Dec 1918. **(Navy Department Library)**

Publication of a newsletter from time to time by crews of U.S. Navy ships was an approved activity. The crew of the *Nebraska* issued, *The Mariner—published by the crew of the U.S.S. Nebraska "for the good of the ship,"* on a monthly basis from January through December 1918. Later the subtitle was changed slightly to

"Published by the crew on board their ship, the U.S.S. NEBRASKA, "For the good of the ship." Chief Lee (author of *Anthem Nebraska*) was the editor. Only the January issue featured a table of contents;

MORALE, by Commander I. A. Cotton, USN…

AN APPRECIATION OF THE N.N.V., by "L"…

OUR COUNTRY, by Edward Everett Hale…

EDITORIALS…

"THE CHIEF SAYS", by H. N. Dinsmore…

FRANCIS X DILLON, by "L"…

HIS REVERENCE, By Father Foley

REPORT OF THE MARINER SOECIETY…

CAMOUFLAGE, A Poem, By "L"…

The newsletter averaged around 20 pages and covered various topics relevant to the crew and included paid commercial advertisements. It was available for .15 cents per copy or $1.50 per year. One important feature of the publication was the ship's sports teams. Commander Coontz had talked about the champion baseball and football teams the *Nebraska* had, and although not winners every year, by 1918 they still fielded teams to be reckoned with. Part of the sports column in the April issue was aimed at encouraging "new men on the ship,"

> *"In 1908 we won the baseball trophy at Melbourne, Australia on the around-the-world cruise. In 1913, 1914 and 1915 the Nebraska won first place for the fleet championship. In 1916 we held third place…now with the advent of the 1918 season we want nothing short of the trophy and a pedestal will be made so that it may occupy a prominent place in our trophy case on the halfdeck. If you are a member of the team, play clean base-ball…put your whole heart into the game, that's what counts! If you are a rooter (and that means a great majority of the ship's company) get behind the team and root, root, root!…last fall at the close of the last game for the divisional baseball championship, defeated though we were of the three hard and grueling contests, the entire ship's company formed behind the squad and with banners flying*

and the band playing "Anchors Aweigh", we marched back to the river. This was commented upon by many officers of high rank who were present..."

The USS Nebraska's 1912 baseball team. Their caps are adorned with the letter 'N' and the word Nebraska is printed down the front of their jerseys. (U.S. Naval Historical Center)

A column in the November issue called, "Sick Bay Cut-Ups," had the byline, "By Old Doc Newmonia," and answered all kinds of health concerns. A portion of the article was dedicated to "Dr. New Monia's Health Column", "Will answer questions which will aid in relieving the suffering of humanity." Some of the questions were apparently of an embarrassing nature, for example, "Dear Docter, Please give me a recipe for the [lightning] of body hair" and "I swallowed a silver dollar..." The ship was active in humanitarian aims as this boxed item also from the November issue illustrates,

> *"Christmas for the Kiddies. It has been a custom for the crew of the Nebraska to donate a fund for the kiddies of Boston every year. This year they will need it more than any other so every body help to make this Christmas fund a grand success."*

One could easily assume the higher need "This year" that was mentioned referred to the horrible Flu Epidemic of 1918.

An editorial in the August 1918 issue regarding smokers (informal social gatherings) held on board revealed what the crew had nicknamed their ship, "A smoker is a good thing anywhere, but a smoker on the NEBBY, Oh! that's different."

Battleship Nebraska on New York's Hudson River in 1911. The funnel bands indicate her place in her assigned division. (U.S. Naval Historical Center)

After leaving drydock, she trained Armed Guard Crews in the Chesapeake Bay Area and at sea until April 1918. The ship underwent repairs once again during five days in April, at the Norfolk Navy Yard this time, and on May 16, received on board the body of the late Carlos Maria De Pena, Envoy Extraordinary and Minister Plenipotentiary from Uruguay, with full honors. The ship departed for Uruguay the same day, and 15 days later arrived in Bahia, Brazil for coal. June 4 found the *Nebraska* at Rio de Janeiro, and on June 10, arriving at Montevideo, Uruguay, with the U.S. Pacific Fleet flagship *Pittsburgh*. After holding quarters for honors and firing 21-gun national salutes on two occasions, she docked. The Commander-in-Chief of the Pacific Fleet came aboard for the ceremonies and the body of the late Uruguayan Minister to the United States was transferred with full honors. *Nebraska* returned to Hampton Roads, Virginia on July 26, 1918.[2]

After another stop for repairs at the Boston Navy Yard, she departed New York on September 17, as principal escort for a fast merchant convoy of 18 ships to an eastern Atlantic rendezvous. By this time, the ship had received a startling camouflage paint job. Known as "dazzle camouflage," the entire vessel was painted in a design of white, gray and black angles which was called Norfolk Design No. 3, and its purpose was to confuse submarine commanders and range finders.[3]

Nebraska, during WWI, in her "dazzle camouflage" which was intended to confuse enemy range-finders. (U.S. Naval Historical Center)

On October 5, 1918, command of the *Nebraska* was transferred from Captain Burrage to Captain D. W. Wurtsbaugh. On October 13, she left New York with the *Montana* and HMS *Edinburgh* as escort for a mercantile convoy of twelve

British ships bound for Liverpool, England, until intercepted by the Eastern Atlantic escort. She returned to Hampton Roads on October 30. On November 13, along with the *Talbot* and HMS *Teutonic*, she left New York on her last wartime convoy escort duty.

Nebraska docked at Boston July 1919. By this time all casemate guns had been removed from Virginia class battleships. The New Jersey is on the far side. (**U.S. Naval Historical Center**)

After the war ended, *Nebraska* began returning troops from Brest, France. She returned to Newport News, Virginia on January 28, 1919, from the first trip, with 1,029 troops. The second trip ended on March 10, at Boston, with 982 troops. Returning to Virginia after her third trip on May 1, she disembarked 1,240 troops. Her fourth and final trip ended at Newport News on June 21, with 1,279 troops. By mid-year, the *Nebraska* safely returned over 4,500 doughboys to their home soil.

Postcard showing USS Nebraska in the locks at Pedro Miguel, Panama Canal 1919. (Author's collection)

In late June 1919, the ship was assigned to Division 2, Squadron One, U.S. Pacific Fleet, to serve on the west coast under the command of Captain P. N. Olmstead.

On July 2, 1920, the USS *Nebraska* was decommissioned at San Francisco, California. Fifteen days later, the Navy Department officially adopted an alphanumeric designation system for identification of battleships as "BB," starting with the USS *Indiana* (commissioned in 1895) as BB-1. Since the *Nebraska* was the fourteenth battleship to be built, it was retroactively designated BB-14.[4] Although much of today's literature refers to these ships by their 'BB' designations, those decommissioned before the adoption of this system were never known by that during their service.

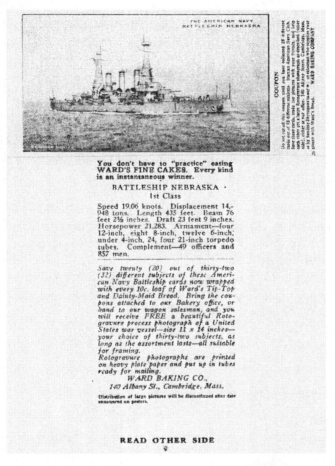

"The American Navy Battleship Nebraska." One of 32 different bread coupons featuring U.S. Naval ships which were produced by the Ward Baking Company, Cambridge, MA. Coupons were included in every 10-cent bread loaf and when 20 different coupons were collected, the customer could turn them in for an 11x14" Rotogravure photograph of the ship of his or her choice. (Front and back of coupon pictured.)
(Author's collection)

The battleship *Nebraska* languished dockside for three more years before being sold for scrap on November 30, 1923. She was one of the many ships disposed of by the Navy under the requirements of the Washington Naval Arms Limitation Treaty of 1922.[5] After 13 years of service, the nearly $7,000,000 battleship was sold for $37,100 to Lemer & Rosenthal, scrap metal dealers from Oakland, California. Dismantling was conducted at the Mare Island Navy Yard.[6]

The entire *Virginia* class of battleships was retired at this time, with the *Georgia* and *Rhode Island* also being scrapped. The *Virginia* and *New Jersey* met an inglorious end when they were sunk for training purposes by Army Air Service bombers off Diamond Shoals, N.C.

Faced with the prospect of scrapping several battleships, the immensity of the task at hand was discovered to be one that never had been undertaken. The United States realized it had no experience in scrapping what was the original series of modern armored battleships built by this country. The March 1922 issue of *Scientific American* featured a technical story on the problem, "At the suggestion and with the assistance of the Navy Department, we are publishing the present article for the purpose of making prospective bidders for these ships broadly familiar with the problem." It outlined the suggested steps one would take in basically disassembling a battleship with the oxy-acetylene torch which had mostly replaced the labor-intensive cold chisel used by scrap yards. One of the first steps was to torch off sections of the gun barrels, rendering them useless. A topic of some fascination, articles on the huge scrapping process also appeared that summer in *Collier's* and *The Literary Digest*.

A melancholy photo of the USS Nebraska being scrapped at Mare Island CA, Navy Yard. A first step in the process was to torch off the gun barrels. **(Author's collection)**

On August 24, 1922, after a request from Governor Samuel McKelvie, *Nebraska's* impressive silver service was returned to the state and housed in the Governor's Mansion. A Navy Department letter explained the condition of the transfer, "…*the silver service of the old battleship Nebraska was loaned to the state of Nebraska.*"

Governor Roy Cochran received a letter dated February 3, 1936, from the Secretary of the Navy, requesting the return of the silver service,

> "*There is no silver service on board the cruiser Omaha and inasmuch as this vessel will soon be assigned as a flagship, it is considered very desirable that she will carry a silver service that will create a favorable impression, and the Department would appreciate the return of the above silver service to Navy custody so that it might be placed on the Omaha.*"

The secretary included a government bill of lading for shipment of the silver service addressed to "the Officer in Charge Naval Supply Depot San Diego California marked for U.S.S. Omaha." An Omaha advertising executive was in contact with the Governor's wife by letter during the latter part of February when he was asked by the historical society to furnish her with certain relative information. John P. Ridgway was a native Nebraskan who told her, "it was my privilege to serve on this ship (*Nebraska*)," and agreed with her and the Governor that, "the silver service from the U.S.S. Nebraska rightfully belongs in the Executive Mansion."[7] He offered to assist in raising funds in Omaha for a new service for the cruiser.

Governor Cochran didn't answer the Navy's letter until April 14, during which he reminded the secretary that when the state received the service, "…four sterling silver punch cups and one large sterling silver loving cup was missing." He further stated that,

> *"For years this silver service has been used in the Governor's Mansion where every year it is viewed and enjoyed by thousands of Nebraskans…I am speaking for the majority of the citizens of Nebraska when I say that we would like to keep this silver here…"*

The Governor, somewhat on the offensive, brazenly went on to ask the Navy's assistance in retrieving missing pieces;

> *"Last spring the silver tea service which was used on the battleship Nebraska was sold at auction in San Francisco for about $800. Why was Nebraska not notified that this silver was to be disposed of? Will it be possible for you to help our State locate the silver and try to bring it back to Nebraska where we feel it belongs? Also, will you help us locate the five missing pieces which were not returned in 1922? The firm who ordered the silver originally, say it would cost around $20,000 to duplicate it."*

Obviously feeling that a strong offense was the best defense, Governor Cochran intentionally let the Navy Department know of his dismay in that agency's mishandling, and subsequent loss of part of the service. One might assume that the Navy didn't want to pursue the can of worms that seemed to be opening up on the subject and dropped its pursuit of the service.

There also seems to be a disagreement on the original cost of the service. Early records mention $3,000 in state funds were appropriated for the purchase. A successor to one of the original owners of Smith & Co. estimated that at the price of silver in 1905, with the labor involved, the initial cost of the service must have been $10,000. The company mentioned in a 1905 letter that it hoped to benefit from good advertising as, "it is all glory and no profit." Interestingly, in the 1936 correspondence, Governor Cochran told the Navy that the original firm that had produced it said it would cost $20,000 to duplicate it. What would that value be in 2005?

The silver service continued to be used for state dinners at the Governor's Mansion for many years. It had been used, damaged, repaired, polished and cleaned and finally retired for display. In 1999, the Gerald R. Ford Conservation Center (a division of the Nebraska State Historical Society) in Omaha performed a complete restoration which included making appropriate structural repairs, cleaning and applying a protective coating to negate tarnishing.[8] The service is currently on display in the formal dining room in the Governor's Mansion.

It seems all good stories include a mystery and the story of the battle-ship *Nebraska* is no exception. Apparently, the bow ornament which the state requested, and received from the Navy, is missing. The state historical society did in fact receive it and store it, as evidence shows from the 1909 annual report, but what happened to it in the meantime remains a mystery. It's unlikely someone would walk off with 4,000 pounds of cast iron without being noticed. An article by staff writer James Denney appeared in the February 28, 1988, issue of the *Omaha World Herald*, which publicized the mystery. James A. Hanson, then director of the state historical society, explained two rumors in the article regarding the ornament's whereabouts; that it's buried under the state capitol; and that it's buried under the parking lot at the corner of 16th and H Streets, southeast of the capitol. He offered one other possibility however, that it was given up for scrap drives during World War II. Considering the comment made by the society in 1909 when they received the ornament, *"…cannot be exhibited until we have more room,"* one might entertain the notion of a donation for the war effort. But, one wouldn't reasonably think that the collections of a state historical society, whose purpose is to preserve historical artifacts, would be an acceptable source for a scrap drive. Additionally, if it was given up for this purpose, or any other, one would expect a record of its disposal to exist. Hopefully one day, the mystery will be solved.

Robert E. Coontz, the Nebraska's first executive officer, served the Navy for more than 43 years. In 1919, he was selected as the second Chief of Naval Operations. **(U.S. Naval Historical Center)**

The life and naval career of Robert E. Coontz, *Nebraska's* first executive officer (second in command), was quite remarkable and worth mentioning here. Coontz grew up in Hannibal, Missouri, and lived near the family of Samuel Clemens, also known as Mark Twain. In fact, Coontz' parents went to school with the literary genius. At a young age, he dreamed of becoming a naval officer. Coontz applied to Congressman William Henry Hatch (he sponsored the law creating the office of Secretary of Agriculture) and after winning an elimination contest, entered the United States Naval Academy in 1881. He graduated from the Naval Academy June 5, 1885 standing 28th in a class of 36. Holding the rating of "Passed Midshipman" for 2 years, he was made Ensign in 1887, and earned $83 per month.

He served aboard various ships including the *Mohican, the Juniata, the Galena* and for a short time, the famous *Constitution*. In February 1888, he was transferred to Sitka, Alaska where the Navy maintained a force "for protection from

Indians." By 1896, he was serving aboard the *Philadelphia* at San Diego and then on to the *Charleston* which saw service at Manila during the Spanish-American War. After his service on the *Nebraska*, he was assigned to the Naval Academy, where he later became Commandant of Midshipmen. From 1912 to 1913, he served as Governor of Guam. He received his first sea command on the *Georgia* from 1913–1915. He was then appointed as Commandant, Navy Yard, Puget Sound, Washington. He became Commander of the Seventh Division, United States Fleet in 1918, and assistant for Naval Operations. He was awarded the Distinguished Service Medal (DSM) for exceptionally meritorious service in the duty of Commandant of the 13th Naval District at Bremerton, Washington. In September 1919, Admiral Coontz was selected to become the second Chief of Naval Operations (the highest position in the Navy), an appointment he held until mid-1923, when he took the post of Commander in Chief of the U.S. Fleet. In 1925, he led the fleet on a cruise across the Pacific to visit New Zealand and Australia, the first mass deployment of American battleships since the "Great White Fleet." Admiral Coontz served as Commandant of the 5th Naval District until his retirement after 47 years of naval service in 1928. In addition to the DSM, he was awarded the Spanish Campaign Medal, Philippine Campaign Medal, Mexican Service Medal and Victory Medal with the Atlantic Fleet clasp. Coontz published his memoirs in 1930, *From the Mississippi to the Sea*, which included his time on the *Nebraska*. After a series of heart attacks, Coontz died on January 26, 1935. His second book, *True Anecdotes of an Admiral*, was published the same year. The Navy went on to honor him with three ships bearing his name. In April 1944, the troopship *Robert E. Coontz* was launched.[9] Later the USS *Coontz* DLG-9 (later DDG-40), and USS *Admiral R. E. Coontz* AP-122 were added to the Navy's fleet.[10]

Although Admiral Coontz could have been buried in Arlington National Cemetery, his wishes were to be buried in Mount Olivet Cemetery at his hometown of Hannibal, Missouri, with the Veterans of Foreign Wars (of which he was a past Commander-in-Chief) in charge of services. Masonic funeral rites were held in Bremerton before the body traveled via the Burlington Railroad to Missouri. On Friday, February 1, 1935 businesses and public buildings in Hannibal were closed by a proclamation of the mayor so the funeral could be attended, and to honor the Admiral. The services were attended by the Governor, senators and various members of military command staff. Two squadrons of airplanes, one each of the Army and Navy, flew over the graveside services. A detachment of naval militia from St. Louis and a battery of artillery from Mexico, Missouri were also in attendance.

The local newspaper ran many articles about Admiral Coontz' career and the plans for the funeral. One such article was an interview with Russell C. Arthur of Hannibal, who had served under Coontz on the battleship *Nebraska*. Arthur was one of the original crewmen on the ship shortly after construction was completed and made the famous round-the-world cruise. He told the newspaper, "Admiral Coontz, then Lieutenant Commander Coontz, was very fond of his home city, Hannibal, and shortly after I began serving on the battleship *Nebraska*, he found out that I lived in Hannibal and I know that this fact helped." He went on to tell more about Coontz:

> *"Admiral Coontz was really a wonderful man. He appreciated a good joke, and he knew how to tell one. When he gave a command he meant it and saw that it was obeyed. The men all respected him because they knew that he was absolutely just…and we who knew him so well and had served under him, admired him for his many virtues, his kindly deeds, his patriotism, his real fighting ability and his absolute fairness in dealing with his fellow man."*

It may be somewhat surprising for visitors that the Admiral's gravestone is a modest U. S. Government military issue marked simply, "ROBERT EDWARD COONTZ MISSOURI ADMIRAL U. S. NAVY DSM JANUARY 26, 1935."

Four months after Admiral Coontz' funeral, the State Historical Society of Missouri erected two bronze markers in Hannibal's Central Park. One was for former Congressman William Henry Hatch and the other for Admiral Robert E. Coontz.

Later a larger marker was placed not far from the grave that featured his name, dates of birth and death, and his likeness. It reads:

> *"Born and raised in Hannibal, he received his appointment to Naval Academy by Congressman Wm. Henry Hatch, and graduated in 1885. He spent the next 43 years in the Navy. He rose from Cadet at Annapolis to Chief of Naval Operations, the highest rank in the Navy. He served aboard the Pinta, Charleston, Enterprise, Philadelphia, Nebraska, Georgia, Nevada, and commanded the 7th Div. Atlantic Fleet aboard the flagship Wyoming. Finally in 1923 he was made Commander in Chief of the U. S. Fleet aboard the Seattle. His accomplishments in the Navy and after retirement are too numerous to mention on this memorial, but with all his fame, Hannibal was always his home."*

The citizens of Hannibal continued to honor Coontz. On November 4, 1939 a new building was dedicated in the town. Built by the Works Progress Administration (WPA) of locally quarried stone, it measured 180 x 100, and would double as the headquarters of Company L, 138th Infantry, Missouri National Guard, and as a community center. It was named, "Admiral Robert E. Coontz Armory."[11]

The construction of the battleship *Nebraska* in Seattle was such a milestone in the history of that city's progress, that it was celebrated 100 years after its launching. In October 2004, Seattle's Museum of History & Industry (MOHAI) commemorated the centennial of the event with a special program by local maritime scholar Tiger Avery.[12] The MOHAI's lobby is home to a scale model of the Moran Brothers shipyard, including a miniature USS *Nebraska*.

Chapter 5

Diving-boats to Boomers

To fully appreciate the technologically-advanced submarines serving the United States today, including the USS *Nebraska* SSBN-739, we should take a brief look at their development over the past 200 years.

Although designs and experiments with primitive submersibles had been conducted in the 1500s, the first operational military submersible was designed by Yale University student David Bushnell in 1776. Bushnell used it to deliver underwater mines that he was working on. His boat, the *Turtle*, was a wooden, egg shaped affair, operated by one man. The sailor hand cranked a screw for propulsion. It was equipped with an external drill bit which was to make a hole in an enemy's wooden hull where a time bomb could be attached. During the night of September 6, 1776, a Continental soldier, Sergeant Ezra Lee, piloted the *Turtle* into New York harbor. He approached the HMS *Eagle*, the flagship of the Royal Navy blockading force, commanded by Admiral Lord Howe, and attempted to place a bomb on its hull. Unable to attach it, he proceeded back to shore being chased by British soldiers in a rowboat. He released the bomb which exploded, scaring, but not injuring the pursuers.[1] The first war-time engagement by a submarine didn't produce anything except the promise of future success.

The American designer, Robert Fulton, who was later famous for his development of steam-ships, improved on the *Turtle*. His submarine, *Nautilus*, launched in May of 1800, towed a bomb which was exploded under the hull of an obsolete ship at Brest, France, utterly destroying it. Monsieur St. Aubin inspected the *Nautilus* and his report appeared in the *Naval Chronicle* of July 1802. He described the "diving-boat", as;

> *"being spacious enough to contain 8 men and provisions*
> *enough for 20 days, and will be of sufficient strength and*

power to enable him to plunge 100 feet under water, if nec-
essary. He has contrived a reservoir for air, which will enable
8 men to remain under water for 8 hours. When the boat is
above water, it has two sails and looks just like a common
boat. When she is to dive, the mast and sails are struck...per-
haps in a few years hence we will not be surprised to see a flo-
tilla of diving-boats, which on a given signal, shall, to avoid
the pursuit of an enemy, plunge underwater, and rise again
several leagues from the place where they descended...with
these qualities it is fit for carrying secret orders to succour a
blockaded port and to examine the force and position of an
enemy."

Regarding the demonstration and ultimate destruction of the ship at Brest, St. Aubin makes this prophetic observation;

"and if by future experiments, the same effect could be pro-
duced on frigates or ships of the line, what will become of
maritime wars, and where will sailors be found to man ships
of war, when it is a physical certainty that they may every
moment be blown into the air by means of a Diving-boat,
against which no human foresight can guard them."

Fulton was awarded a contract from the French, but was turned down by the British. The rejection from the British may have been because he was an American but probably because the method of an unseen vessel attacking another without warning was looked upon as villainous. He then returned to America where he went to work on his steam-ship designs.

The first sinking of a warship by a submarine occurred during the Civil War. Confederate engineer, Horace L. Hunley, built the submarine CSS *Hunley*, which carried a commander and eight men (who cranked the propeller). During trials, the submarine sank five different times killing a total of 41 sailors, including its inventor! Apparently still sold on the whole idea, it was raised again and a new crew found. On February 17, 1864, the *Hunley* attacked the sloop USS *Housatonic* in Charleston harbor.[2] A spar-torpedo was used which blew a hole in the sloop's hull below the waterline. Five Union sailors died in the blast and the sloop sunk within minutes. It is believed that the explosion swamped the *Hunley* sinking it also, at a cost of nine more lives. This was its last mission. The engagement had a profound effect on naval warfare however, and the submarine was here to stay. In 1995, the location of *Hunley's* watery grave was discovered and the historic submarine was raised in 2000.

On February 24, 1842, John P. Holland was born in an Irish coastal village. At 17 he drew up plans for a boat that would be propelled underwater. He became a schoolmaster but his first love continued to be the sea. Like so many Irish families, the Hollands immigrated to America. By 1875, he found financial backing and proposed a submarine design to the secretary of the Navy. The design was forwarded to Captain Edward Simpson at the Naval War College in Rhode Island who rejected Holland's idea saying he doubted if sailors could be found who were willing to serve underwater. Reminding the captain that the Confederate navy had no trouble finding volunteers did nothing to change the officer's mind. Two years later, Holland found backing by Irish patriots called the Fenians, who were interested in using the submarine against the British. Members of the group stole his 30-foot submarine, *Fenian Ram,* because they didn't believe the inventor had strong enough anti-British goals.[3] Today, the *Fenian Ram* is on display at the Paterson Museum in Paterson, NJ.

In 1888, under President Grover Cleveland's administration, the Navy secretary secured $150,000, with which to advertise for designs and bids for a submarine. None of the designs submitted were approved but the following year, Holland's design was chosen. Unfortunately, a new president was elected who appointed a new secretary of the Navy. The secretary had no interest in submarines and used the allotted funds in other areas.

The U.S. Navy's budget for 1893–94 included $200,000 for the construction of an experimental submarine. Holland finally was awarded the contract which resulted in the operational submarine *Plunger.* The vessel was mostly a success, but the design needed further work. A deal was made with American businessman Isaac Rice who incorporated the Electric Boat Company in February 1899, absorbing the Holland Torpedo Boat Company, the Electro-Dynamic Company and the Electric Launch Company. The result of this team was the *Holland* which completed sea trials in 1899. The submarine was 54-feet long and displaced 75 tons. A gasoline engine powered her on the surface and an electric motor while submerged. It was the first to recharge its own batteries. The *Holland* was fitted with a single torpedo tube in the bow. The first production model was 63-feet long, and was fitted with a 160-horsepower engine. It was purchased by the U.S. Navy in 1900 for $150,000, the first to be added to the fleet. It added six more of Holland's submarines in the following years. The Royal Navy also purchased rights to build the sub for its own fleet.

The period before World War I saw great expansion in submarine fleets, especially in Great Britain and Germany. Many advances were made including the diesel engine, wireless communication and periscopes. Submarines were larger and equipped with multiple torpedo tubes fore and aft. In September, 1914, shortly after the start of World War I, the German navy defined the potential of submarine warfare. The *U-9* (Undersea boat #9), sank three British cruisers in one day.

Within five years of the end of the war, the Navy had 113 submarines of the 'O', 'R' and 'S' class. Because of old designs and technology (submarine science progressed rapidly at this time) many were scrapped. The U.S. Navy experienced yet another period of dormancy between the world wars. The revival, albeit late, was spurred by the Imperial Japanese Navy when it attacked the naval base at Pearl Harbor, Hawaii. At the start of World War II, the U.S. Navy still had 64 obsolete submarines. A modern submarine was needed to support fleet activities in the vast Pacific Ocean. After Pearl Harbor, there wasn't much of a fleet to support however, and the submarine service and the aircraft carriers became the Navy's primary offense. Along with the 1920's 'S' class boats, ten boats of the *Porpoise* class were built in the mid-thirties. This was the force on December 7, 1941.

America's war production shifted quickly into overdrive however. The *Gato* and *Balao* class boats were the successful workhorses of the war. The *Gato*, 312 feet long, displacing 2,420 tons, was powered by four diesel engines that produced 2,720 horsepower submerged and could dive to 300 feet. It featured six bow torpedo tubes, and four in the stern as well as a deck gun. The *Balao*, virtually an improved *Gato*, could dive to 400 feet because of a stronger hull. By the end of the war, the 73 *Gatos*, 132 *Balao*, and 31 *Tench* class boats (another improved model) sank a large share of the Japanese war and merchant ships lost by that country.

The war with Japan ended as a result of new weapon technology, atomic bombs. Captain Hyman G. Rickover (later Admiral) was one of the first to realize the potential of atomic power for submarines. In conjunction with the Navy, the Argonne National Laboratory and Westinghouse, the Submarine Thermal Reactor was developed. Congress authorized the first nuclear-powered boat, USS *Nautilus* SSN-571, in 1952, and construction was completed in 1954. (SS means submarine, N is nuclear-powered). *Nautilus* made history in 1958, when it left Hawaii and transited the polar ice cap. The USS *Halibut* SSGN-587 was commissioned in January 1960 and two months later it became the first nuclear submarine to launch a guided missile. It was equipped with a Regulus 1 missile, armed with a 45 kt warhead and had a 500-mile range. The Regulus program however, was cancelled to concentrate on the new Polaris weapons. Great progress with nuclear-powered submarines continued during that year. The USS *Triton* SSN-586, the only submarine powered by two reactors, was the first to circumnavigate the earth submerged, taking 84 days. The famed WWII submariner and naval author, Captain Edward L. Beach commanded the *Triton*. The route followed was the one taken by explorer Ferdinand Magellan's expedition during the three-year voyage, 1519–1522.

With the Cold War in full swing, the U.S. was interested in the possibility of arming submarines with sea-launched ballistic missiles (SLBM). A strong deterrent against an enemy first strike was needed and nuclear submarines seemed to be the answer. A Skipjack class attack submarine was converted to carry 16 Polaris missiles abaft the sail and was launched in June 1959, as the USS *George Washington* SSBN-598. The Navy's system designates a missile submarine as "SSBN" (Submarine Ballistic Missiles Nuclear-powered).

On July 20, 1960, the *George Washington* successfully fired two missiles while submerged. The *Ethan Allen, Lafayette* and *Benjamin Franklin* class boats followed. In 1970, the USS *James Madison* launched the new Poseidon missile, which had the same range as the Polaris, but was equipped with three more warheads. The last Poseidon missiles had a range of 2,878 miles, but the Navy wanted a longer range capability. Enter the Trident C-4, the third generation of SLBMs.

A new ballistic missile submarine was designed to accommodate the Trident, which began construction in 1976 at the General Dynamics Electric Boat Division in Groton, Connecticut. The first of the massive *Ohio* class, USS *Ohio* SSBN-726, was commissioned on November 11, 1981. With a stated hull life of 42 years, it should last until 2023. The submarine is 560 feet long, making it longer than the Washington Monument is tall (for Nebraska Cornhuskers, it is 160 feet longer than the tower of the State Capitol), with a 42-foot beam (width) and displaces a whopping 18,750 tons. It was equipped with 24 Trident C-4 missiles, each with a range of 4,000 miles. It also features Mk 48 torpedoes fired through four bow torpedo tubes. The *Ohio* class was originally planned to consist of 24 boats, but with arms limitation agreements and the collapse of the Soviet Union, only 18 would be built, all by Electric Boat (EB). On March 12, 1998, the *Ohio* celebrated its 50th strategic patrol.[4] These missile submarines serve in both the Atlantic and Pacific fleets. The first four of the class, *Ohio, Michigan, Florida* and *Georgia,* currently are undergoing conversion from missile boats to guided missile launching platforms (SSGNs).

The historic Electric Boat Company, with its start in the 1890s, sold submarines around the globe. John P. Holland left the company in 1904, after numerous skirmishes with managers. He believed the company only was interested in selling a product and not in advancing the technology. The man known as the inventor of the submarine died in 1914. During World War I, Electric Boat built 85 submarines for the U.S. Navy, the last one being delivered in 1925. The USS *Cuttlefish,* delivered in 1934, was the first boat ordered since the WWI contracts and was the first welded submarine. It was built at the company's new Groton, Connecticut shipyard. The company continued to expand and acquire other businesses and facilities. During WWII, EB built 74 submarines, 398 PT boats and other war materiel. The first nuclear-powered submarine, USS *Nautilus* SSN-571, and the first submarine to surface at the North Pole, USS *Skate* SSN-578, were also products of EB. In the mid-1970s, the Newport News Shipbuilding & Drydock Company and Electric Boat began construction of the new *Los Angeles* class of nuclear attack submarines. The two would build the entire class of 62 boats. Electric Boat added the vacated Quonset Point Naval Air Station in Rhode Island to its facilities in 1974 where it developed a mass production construction plant that would significantly reduce the time it took to build a submarine. Cylindrical hull sections are built at the new facility, known as the Automated Submarine Frame and Cylinder Manufacturing Facility, and then transported to Groton where the boats are assembled section by section.

A 1,200 ton hull section of the USS Wyoming (SSBN-742) is delivered to Electric Boat's Groton, CT shipyard from EB's Quonset Point, RI facility in this undated photo. (**General Dynamics Electric Boat**)

The high-quality construction and dependability that Electric Boat has become known for led to the company's winning of the contract for the new *Seawolf* class submarines and has partnered with Newport News Shipbuilding (now owned by Northrop Grumman) in construction of the *Virginia* class submarines.

Chapter 6

"Big Red"—Defender of Peace

During the late 1960s, the Navy decided to name new guided missile cruisers after states. In 1971, Clint Orr of Omaha, a World War II submariner, sent letters to then Governor J. James Exon Jr., asking him to have a resolution passed in the Legislature that one of the new frigates be named after the state of Nebraska.[1] Exon had the wheels in motion and the request was forwarded to Senator Roman Hruska, who in turn sent it to the Navy Department. The state was not successful in getting another warship named after it at that time, but when construction began on the new fleet of Trident submarines, the campaign began anew.

On December 16, 1987, the *Omaha World Herald* ran a news release from then Senator Exon, a member of the Senate Armed Services Committee (and the Strategic Forces and Nuclear Deterrence Subcommittee) by that time, which stated that a new Trident submarine would carry the name *Nebraska*. Two days later Secretary of the Navy James H. Webb Jr., made the formal announcement, "SSBNs 736, 737, 738, and 739 will be named for the states of West Virginia, Kentucky, Maryland and Nebraska respectively."

By 1992, thirteen *Ohio* class missile submarines had been added to the U.S. Navy's inventory. The *Nebraska* BB-14 was the 14th battleship to be built, and coincidentally, the USS *Nebraska* SSBN-739 submarine was the 14th in its class to be built. On Christmas Eve, 1987, the keel of the *Nebraska* was laid at the General Dynamics Electric Boat Division at Groton.

At a May 29, 1992, news conference, Senator J. James Exon Jr., Charles M. Harper, Chairman and CEO of ConAgra, and Harold W. Andersen, former publisher of the *Omaha World Herald*, launched a statewide effort to commemorate the christening and commissioning of the new submarine. Captain William R. Hansell and six members of the sub's 165-man crew were present, before going on to visit Omaha, Lincoln, Grand Island, North Platte and Kearney. One of the statewide activities planned by the steering committee was handled by the Society of Nebraska Admirals. They supervised the flying of three flags, the U.S., state of Nebraska, and the Q125 (1992 was the state's 125th anniversary) over all 93 county courthouses in the state. The three flags then were presented to the ship at its christening.

On August 15, 1992, she was launched. The *Rhode Island*, nearing completion, towered over the ceremony on a dry dock beside the *Nebraska*. The visitors were able to see the size of the entire Trident submarine, which is difficult to grasp when in the water. Members of the Committee, the Society of Nebraska Admirals, and the Nebraska-Wahoo Chapter U.S. Submarine Veterans of WWII were seated just opposite the speaker's platform which was on the submarine.

Launching ceremonies for the Nebraska (SSBN-739) on August 15, 1992 at Groton, CT. Note the massive size of sister ship Rhode Island in the background. (**Submarine Force Museum**)

Sponsor Patricia Pros Exon (Senator Exon's wife) stated, "I christen thee, *Nebraska*," as she smashed the bottle of champagne against the sail formally christening the new ship. For the first time in more than 70 years, a U.S. Navy vessel carried the name of the Cornhusker State. The program for the day included music by the Navy Band from Newport, RI. Roger E. Tetrault, President of Electric Boat Division, gave the welcome to guests and dignitaries. He was followed to the podium by the Executive Vice President of General Dynamics Corporation, James E. Turner, Jr. Then Governor of the State of Nebraska, E. Benjamin Nelson, offered his greetings to the crowd, followed by Rear Admiral Michael Coyle, Deputy Commander for Submarines, and the Honorable Christopher J. Dodd, U. S. Senator from Connecticut. Vice Admiral Roger F. Bacon, Assistant Chief of Naval Operations for Undersea Warfare introduced the principle speaker, the Honorable James J. Exon Jr., U.S. Senator (and past governor) from Nebraska. The $2 billion-dollar *Nebraska* was the 200th submarine built by Electric Boat during its long history.

Carrying on a tradition that began in 1904 with the launching of the battleship, an entourage of Nebraska dignitaries traveled to Groton, Connecticut, for the launching of the submarine. The Steering Committee that was formed to assist with the preparations for this auspicious occasion included the co-chairmen, the Coordinator, James M. McCoy, and the following Committee Members:

Red Abels	CDR Dennis A. Hathaway
Dale Andersen	Richard E. Holloway
Allen Beermann	Lenore Honke
Mark Bowen	Lloyd L. Johnson
Dick Cleary	Shirley J. Kuhle
Chuck Clifford	CAPT Norman A. Marks
Richard Dohrman	Gerald D. McDonald
Dan Dube	Scott R. Micheels
Gary Gates	Clint Orr
Jeff Gauger	Bill Ramsey
John A. Gondring	Roy Roberts
Ivan Griswold	Richard C. Seaman, Sr.
LCDR Thomas Guinn	Gerald Sweet
Barbara Haggart	Gerald M. Swift
Richard Hahn	CAPT Frank Tryon
John Hanlon	Jesse Virant
	David E. Weaver

In the summer of 1993, an estimated 500 Nebraskans made their way to Connecticut again, this time to Naval Submarine Base New London, to take part in the commissioning ceremonies of "their" submarine on July 10th. Celebrations the preceding evening included a reception for the commanding officers and chiefs sponsored by the Society of Nebraska Admirals.

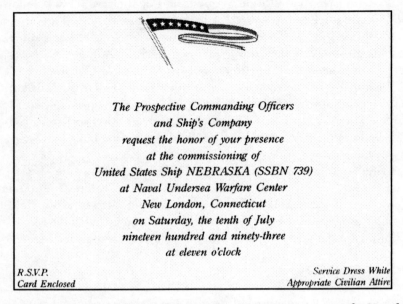

The Prospective Commanding Officers
and Ship's Company
request the honor of your presence
at the commissioning of
United States Ship NEBRASKA (SSBN 739)
at Naval Undersea Warfare Center
New London, Connecticut
on Saturday, the tenth of July
nineteen hundred and ninety-three
at eleven o'clock

R.S.V.P.   Service Dress White
Card Enclosed   Appropriate Civilian Attire

Official invitation to Nebraska's commissioning ceremonies at the Naval Undersea Warfare Center, New London, CT. (Author's collection)

The hour long program began at 11:30 a.m., on Pier No. 7, at the Naval Undersea Warfare Center, with an invocation by Lieutenant Paul E. Roma, CHC, USNR. Welcoming remarks were made by the ship's two commanding officers, Captain William R. Hansell, USN (Blue), and Captain Charles B. Beckman USN (Gold). (The Navy decided later that officers holding the rank of Commander would be eligible for command of missile subs.) Missile submarines have two complete crews, Blue and Gold, which rotate duty on the sub. While one is at sea, the other enjoys some off time and lots of continued training. James E. Turner, Jr., President of Electric Boat Division offered his perspective to the occasion of his company's completion of another Trident submarine. Rear Admiral John F. Shipway, USN, Program Executive Officer, Submarines, then spoke just before Nebraska Governor E. Benjamin Nelson took the podium to officially represent the state. Commissioning was carried out by Vice Admiral Hank Chiles, USN, Commander of the U.S. Atlantic Fleet Submarine Force, by reading the commissioning directive. The national anthem was played as the flags were raised on the ship, at which time Captains Hansell and Beckman assumed command.

The order was given to the crew to set the watch, who proceeded to lay below decks, man the rails, and test the ship's missile hatches, periscopes and rudder. The ship's sponsor, Patricia Pros Exon offered her remarks before Vice Admiral Chiles introduced the principal speaker, Senator J. James Exon. Lieutenant Roma then offered the benediction with the Northeastern Navy Band wrapping up the ceremony. A reception was held immediately following the commissioning where Captains Hansell and Beckman received a silver service for the ship that was donated by Borsheim's Fine Jewelry of Omaha. Other gifts presented to the ship included paintings of Nebraska scenes; a ship's log and photo album; a color photo of the Cornhuskers in action at Memorial Stadium; video tapes of Big Red's greatest victories; a football signed by the entire Cornhusker football team; and CD's from American Gramophone's Chip Davis (Mannheim Steamroller).

The crewmembers of a brand new ship at commissioning are known as "plank owners." It's interesting to note that the commissioning program listed four members of the original crew who were from Nebraska; Lieutenant A. E. Tarrell, Kearney; Chief Petty Officer K. J. Goergen, South Sioux City; Petty Officer 2nd Class M. P. Dishman, Lewellen; and Petty Officer 2nd Class T. C. Blase, Edgar.

U.S. Navy ship insignia, or crests, date back to World War II and were designed by their crews. Crests were not officially adopted by the Navy until the 1950s and must be approved by the Naval Board of Heraldry. The Navy's description of the *Nebraska's* crest is;

> *"The shield features a blue and white globe combined with a submarine to make up the Trident silhouette superimposed within an arrowhead. Its main color is red highlighted with a gold trident spear. Supporting the shield on either side are two corn stalks interlaced with a scroll of blue displaying the motto, "Defensor Pacis", or Defender of Peace. The color red, symbolic of valor in action, is surrounded by a coat of dark blue and gold, the traditional colors of the U. S. Navy. The ship's shield is in the shape of an arrowhead, recalling Nebraska's heritage; Nebraska is the Indian word for the state's major river, the Platte. The submarine silhouette and globe represent USS Nebraska's world-wide mission. The trident symbolizes sea power. Its spike suggest the "depths", a submarine's operating environment. Twin cornstalks highlight the connection of USS Nebraska to her namesake "Cornhusker State".*

The coat of arms is emblazoned upon a white back-ground enclosed within a dark blue oval band. The band is edged in red on the inside and encircled by a gold rope. Two gold stars indicate excellence. In white the inscription "USS NEBRASKA" appears at the top and "SSBN-739" at the bottom."

Official crest of the USS Nebraska (SSBN-739).
(Author's collection)

Command and control of all Trident missile submarines comes from the U.S. Strategic Command (StratCom) headquartered at Offutt Air Force Base in Bellevue, Nebraska (formerly the Strategic Air Command, SAC).

Nebraska was assigned to Submarine Group 10, Naval Submarine Base Kings Bay, Georgia, which is the Atlantic homeport for U.S. ballistic missile submarines. NSB Kings Bay encompasses some 16,000 acres, and is located in Camden County, in southeast Georgia. The history of the base began when the army acquired land in 1954 to construct an ammunition shipping terminal to be used in case of national emergency. The facility was completed in 1958, and placed on inactive ready status. The base featured a concrete and steel wharf that measured 2,000 feet long and 87 feet wide. It had three parallel railroad tracks which allowed the loading of several ships at one time. The base had 47 miles of railroad tracks that ran to earthen covered, concrete munitions storage areas. It never was used for its primary purpose but was used during the Cuban Missile Crisis in 1962, when a U.S. Army Transportation Battalion and 70 small boats were stationed there, and in 1964, to shelter residents from Hurricane Dora.

When the U.S. Navy agreed to withdraw Fleet Ballistic Missile Squadron 16 from its base at Rota, Spain, a new base on the East Coast had to be found. On July 1, 1978, after being transferred from the Army to the Navy, Naval Submarine Support Base Kings Bay was established. On July 6, 1978, the USS *James Monroe* SSBN-622 became the first missile sub to dock at the new base. In 1980, the Secretary of the Navy announced that Kings Bay would be the future home of the new Trident missile submarines. After a nine-year building program was completed, three new commands were located at Kings Bay; the Trident Training Facility (TTF); the Trident Refit Facility (TRF); and the Strategic Weapons Facility, Atlantic (SWFA). On January 15, 1989, the USS *Tennessee* SSBN-734 was the first Trident sub to arrive. Following were the *Pennsylvania, West Virginia, Kentucky, Maryland, Nebraska, Rhode Island, Maine, Wyoming* and in 1997, the last Trident, *Louisiana*, arrived. The sail that was removed from the USS *Bancroft* was dedicated at the main gate of the base, now known as Naval Submarine Base Kings Bay, on April 7, 2000, in commemoration of the 100th anniversary of U.S. submarine forces.

More than 50 Nebraskans made the trip to Kings Bay in 2003, to celebrate the USS *Nebraska's* 10th anniversary in commission. The group toured the *Nebraska* and the base including the submarine museum. A huge barbecue was held that featured Nebraska beef. Later the visitors enjoyed dinner at both the Blue and Gold commanders' homes.

Nebraska undergoing periscope repairs at her base, Naval Submarine Base, Kings Bay, GA The sub's magnetic numbers (739) are displayed only while in port. (Bob Conley, Big Red Sub Club)

In October, the announcement was made by the Navy that the *Nebraska* would be transferred to Naval Submarine Base Bangor (WA). This followed the 2002 transfer of the *Pennsylvania* and *Kentucky* for equalization of the Atlantic and Pacific Trident submarine fleets. Part of the reason for the realignment was the removal from strategic service of four of the oldest Tridents (*Ohio, Florida, Michigan and Georgia*) which are being converted to guided missile submarines. The transfer of naval vessels from base to base might seem innocuous to most people, but they can have a tremendous effect on the area. The move resulted in the loss of approximately 330 military personnel, 200 family members and an annual payroll of about $18 million to the Kings Bay-Camden County economy.[2]

The Nebraska's silver service was donated by Borsheim's Fine Jewelry of Omaha, NE. Note the two signed Cornhusker footballs on display in officers' wardroom. **(Bob Conley, Big Red Sub Club)**

The history of NSB Bangor began in 1942, when it was used to ship munitions to the Pacific Theatre of war. The Navy purchased 7,676 acres of land at the Hood Canal near the town of Bangor for a base. The U.S. Naval Magazine was established on June 5, 1944 (the day before D-Day) and began operations in January 1945. It continued to operate as an ammunition depot through the Korean and Vietnam wars. In 1973, the Navy announced that the depot would become headquarters of the 1st Squadron of Trident missile submarines. The Naval Submarine Base Bangor activated on Feb. 1, 1977. It combined with Naval Station Bremerton in June 2004 to become Naval Base Kitsap.

A tug boat guides the Nebraska away from the dock as she leaves Kings Bay, GA for Naval Base Kitsap, WA., August 2004. **(Naval Submarine Base, Kings Bay, Public Affairs)**

The *Nebraska* sailed out of NSB Kings Bay on August 12, 2004, on a 15,000-mile trip which would take the crew around Cape Horn on their way to Washington State. The commanding officer, Commander Christian Haugen (Gold) later advised that the sub surfaced six times during the voyage, which included once at the equator, where they flew a Nebraska and U.S. flag.

Meanwhile, the Big Red Sub Club and the Nebraska Admirals Association were organizing a trip for members, Nebraska officials and community leaders to meet the sub when it arrived at Bangor. Organizers Allen Beermann (Executive Director of the Nebraska Press Association and past Secretary of State) and his wife Linda were assisted by Randy and Jenny Boldt, all of Lincoln. The group of about 50 met at the Nebraska Air National Guard Base in Lincoln at 7 a.m. on October 19, 2004. Major General Roger P. Lempke, Adjutant General of the Nebraska National Guard, supplied and accompanied a KC-135 tanker aircraft for transporting the group to Washington as part of their on going training exercises. The distinguished group included the Nebraska State Patrol Superintendent, two Nebraska state senators, the Chief Deputy Attorney General of Nebraska, the Nebraska Game & Parks Commission Director and a photo journalist who has worked with *National Geographic* magazine.

At about 10 a.m., the plane landed at Naval Air Station Whidbey Island, Washington. The group boarded a bus that took them to the quaint town of Port Townsend for lunch and then on to a hotel at Silverdale. A banquet that evening featured special guests from the Washington Air National Guard, Kathryn Haugen, wife of Commander Haugen, and newly-appointed Blue Crew commanding officer, Commander John Carter and his wife Cheryl. An additional 25 "transplanted Nebraskans" from Washington joined the group of supporters. Melvin Millsap (Fleet Admiral-Nebraska Admirals Association) and his wife Betty also arrived from Nebraska.

Two tug boats gently push the Nebraska to the NB Kitsap dock after her 15,000 mile trip from the east coast, Oct 2004. (U.S. Navy)

Sailors tie up the massive Nebraska at NB Kitsap. (U.S. Navy)

The following day, October 20, the *Nebraska* was due to arrive after its long voyage. The group was bussed to Naval Base Kitsap for tours of the Trident Training Facility and the Naval Undersea Museum. About 20 members of the group were chosen to travel out on Puget Sound and meet the *Nebraska* as it navigated the Strait of Juan de Fuca on its way to Bangor. They boarded the submarine and rode back with the Gold Crew. The rest of the Nebraska contingent took their seats in rows of chairs dockside. The Navy band was present, as well as the *Nebraska's* Blue Crew, awaiting the arrival. Many of the Gold Crew's family members, wives, children and girlfriends arrived to welcome their loved ones home. After the *Nebraska* was gently guided to the dock by two tug boats, the heavy metal gangway was lifted into place. The winner of the traditional drawing for the "first kiss" competition was announced and he ran onto the gangway to meet his wife. Crew members who didn't have duty disembarked. Commander of Submarine Group Nine, (of which the *Nebraska* was now a part) Rear Admiral Melvin G. Williams, Jr., officially welcomed the submarine, families and the supporters from Nebraska. Admiral Williams recognized Commander Haugen, who stepped off the *Nebraska* for the last time. On December 10th, command of the sub would be transferred from Haugen to Commander Geoffrey G. deBeauclair. After speeches were made, the Nebraskans were divided into groups, and each was then given a fascinating two-hour tour of the submarine. It wasn't difficult to figure out the namesake of this submarine. Gifts of pictures, Husker football memorabilia, a Great Seal of the State of Nebraska, and other items were displayed throughout. A sign in the crew's mess proudly reads, "CORNHUSKER CAFÉ." Directly outside of the ward room, a special glass case was built-in housing a piece of the battleship *Nebraska's* original silver service.

Rear Admiral Melvin G. Williams, Commander, Sub Group Nine,
welcomes the USS Nebraska and guests from the Cornhusker state.
(U.S. Navy)

Another banquet that evening featured speakers Admiral Williams, and Commanders Haugen and Carter. Gifts were presented to the commanders, which included a poster signed by the Nebraska contingent. They were then presented with a commercial popcorn popper for the ship, and a year's supply of Nebraska-grown popcorn. James and Barb Ballard, co-owners of James Arthur Vineyards, of Raymond, Nebraska, gave the entire entourage, including distinguished naval personnel, a bottle of custom-labeled wine produced just for the occasion. Kathy Haugen delighted each of the visiting Nebraskans with a beautifully handmade polished brass napkin ring that featured the dolphin insignia of the submarine service and the words, "USS NEBRASKA SSBN-739." American Gramaphone's Chip Davis, another long-time *Nebraska* supporter, sent along Mannheim Steamroller CDs for all members of the entourage. The group flew back to the Cornhusker State on the 21st, all a bit more proud of "their" sub. The trip later was documented by three members of the group. Dale Crawford, managing editor of the *Wymore Arbor State* featured a two-part article, "The USS Nebraska, defending our way of life," in the Nov. 3, 2004 issue, and Pamela Thompson, editor of *L Lincoln's Premier Lifestyle Magazine*, wrote an article, "Around the Horn," for the December 2004 issue. Vern Goff filmed the event and made VHS and DVD copies available later.

COMPARISONS OF USS *NEBRASKA*
BATTLESHIP & SUBMARINE

	Battleship BB-14	Submarine SSBN-739
Displacement	14,865 tons	18,750 tons
Length	441 ft	560 ft
Width	76 ft	42 ft
Draft	24 ft	36 ft
Total Crew Complement	812	165
Cost	$6,832,796.96	$2 billion
Power	2 coal fired boilers	1 nuclear reactor
Time/Distance Before Refuel	4,000 miles at 10 knots	Every 15 years
Service Life	13 years	42 years expected
Primary Weapon Range	3,000–4,000 yards	6,000 miles

Chapter 7

"Big Red" Pride Runs Deep

There's a lot more to "Big Red" pride in Nebraska than meets the eye. The obvious, is the beautiful state Nebraskans call our own. Known historically as "Where the West Begins," and known nationally as the "Cornhusker State," it is true, *"there is no place like Nebraska."* The great pride in our University of Nebraska National Champion football team has flourished for decades. The drum rolls followed by chants of "Go Big Red!" drown out all other sounds at the games. The air is electrified by the pride of tens of thousands of red-clad fans. Products of every kind are produced and sold with the big red "N."

In the 1990s, "Big Red" pride took on a whole different meaning for Nebraskans. The naming of a U.S. Navy ballistic missile submarine for the state, the first warship to carry the name in a long time, was a proud moment. The submarine inevitably earned the nickname, "Big Red." Pride is something carried in the heart of Nebraskans, and true to form the submarine became another target of their affection. Organizations adopted the sub and countless individuals give time, money, materiel and their contagious enthusiasm in support of the ship, commanders, crews and their families. Here is the story of the organizations and but a *few* of the folks dedicated to "their boat."

In 1931, Lieutenant Governor Theodore W. Metcalf became Acting Governor. To express his favor towards 25 of his prominent friends, he appointed them "Admirals," at which time the "Great Navy of the State of Nebraska" was established.[1] The tradition carried on, and by 1984, a gathering of "Admirals" was held in Kearney, Nebraska, to enjoy a social time together. Two years later the Society of Nebraska Admirals (SONA) was formed under the NebraskaLand Foundation, with a kick-off celebration in Omaha. The Foundation was created in 1962 by Governor Frank Morrison to develop tourism in the state. A newsletter was available to members called *Echoes from Sonar*. By April 1987, bylaws were adopted that explained the purposes of the Society which included: the promotion of tourism in the state; the promotion of Nebraska products; the enhancement of Nebraska's agricultural industry; to seek and save Nebraska's sea; the development and maintenance of ports throughout the state; the enjoyment of fun activities, such as "walking the plank"; the building of Nebraska pride and esprit de corps; the recycling of Nebraska's assets; the enlargement of the flagship fleet of the Nebraska Navy; and the continuance of efforts to have U.S. Naval ships named after Nebraska people and places.

In fact, Nebraska Governors have designated various vessels as Flagships of the state's navy. The USS *Centennial* was built by an instructor and students at Southeast Community College for the Nebraska Centennial in 1967, and was so named by Governor Frank Morrison. It was sailed down the Missouri and Mississippi Rivers to promote the celebration. It was later "berthed" at the Plainsman Museum in Aurora. The WWII minesweeper USS *Hazard*, which is on display at the Freedom Park Navy Museum (see Chapter 9) was designated a flag ship by Governor James J. Exon, Jr. The *Meriwether Lewis*, a U.S. Army Corps of Engineers river dredge, was acquired by Gov. Charles Thone for the state, and drydocked at Brownville. The *Viktoria*, a 28' hydrofoil was given to President Richard Nixon by Soviet leader Leonid Brezhnev in 1972. It was used by the U.S. Fish and Wildlife Service for enforcement duties in the southeast. After being declared surplus property, it was acquired by a volunteer group from Ogallala for use on Lake McConaughy. In 1987, the Society of Nebraska Admirals became part owners in the craft, which was dubbed by Governor Kay Orr as a flagship.

During the 1990s, SONA reorganized into the Nebraska Admirals Association (NAA). Admiralships are still approved by, and issued through, the incumbent Governor (the Honorary Chief Commander of the Fleet) but the requirement for receiving the commission is explained by NAA, "While the practice of awarding commissions to the more or less "prominent" has persisted, a requirement for some meaningful act or service to the state or community has become more and more necessary to obtain an Admiral certificate."

The NAA has been involved with the USS *Nebraska* SSBN-739 from the very beginning. Many members also were members of the Steering Committee. From the Three Flags Over Nebraska Project, supporting the christening and commission of the sub, providing gifts, assisting in the sale of USS *Nebraska* paraphernalia, and the hosting of visiting crew members, the NAA has been, and remains, a vital member of the *Nebraska's* support team network.

It's unknown just exactly how many Admiralships have been awarded over the past 74 years, but everyone will recognize some of the notables who have received them; Presidents F. Roosevelt, Truman, Ford, Reagan, George W. Bush and First Lady Laura Bush, General Douglas MacArthur, Queen Elizabeth II, Martin Luther King III, John Glenn, Bob Hope, Jack Benny, Bing Crosby, Dick Cavett, Johnny Carson and Jerry Lewis.

The NAA officers for the year 2005–2006 are: Melvin Millsap, Fleet Admiral, Broken Bow; Gloria LeDroit, Chief of Staff, Kearney; Guy Miller, Operations Officer, Kearney; Jill Shannon, Public Affairs Officer, Kearney; Eddie Biwer, Quartermaster, Omaha; Janice Weibusch, Historian, Kearney; and Dan LeDroit, Scholarship Officer, Kearney.

In August 1991, the Association established an annual Travel & Tourism Scholarship which is offered to a senior at the University of Nebraska-Kearney. The university is one of the few in the country that offers a travel and tourism major. The scholarship amount during the first years was $150, growing to $1,000 in 2005.

Two months before the *Nebraska* was christened, the Steering Committee brought Captain William Hansell, two other officers, the Chief of the Boat (COB), and three crewmen back to tour the state. The sailors attended the College World Series, the Aksarben horse races and toured Henry Doorly Zoo in Omaha, and StratCom Headquarters in Bellevue. They visited several other towns as well.

In late September 1992, after the sub was christened, seven more crewmen were sponsored for a visit to the state. They were honored by riding in the River City Round Up Parade and attending a Husker football game as well as other tours and visits. The Committee would bring two more groups of sailors back to Nebraska before the submarine was commissioned in July of 1993.

More groups followed into 1994, at which time the Committee members decided to convert to a permanent club and sell memberships to help support the sub and continued crew visits. Appropriately named, the Big Red Sub Club (BRSC) was officially established. A four-tier membership rate was developed, Submariner $17.39, Commander $73.90, Captain $173.90 and Commodore $739.00 that incorporates the *Nebraska's* hull number, 739. Befitting gifts for each level accompany the memberships.

The BRSC officers are currently: Richard Holloway, Garden Ridge, TX, Co-Chairman; Dale Andersen, Omaha, Co-Chairman; Gerald Swift, Omaha, Secretary; Chuck Kaipust, Omaha, Treasurer; Robert Conley, Omaha, Newsletter Editor; Clint Orr, Omaha, Historian; and Ivan Griswold, Omaha, Archivist/Chaplin. Eleven members of the original Steering Committee are active BRSC members.

At the time when the BRSC was established, the seventh group of sailors visited the state. On August 18, 1994, Captain Beckman (Gold) had been relieved by

Commander Melvin G. Williams, Jr. Commander Williams and five members of his crew rode in a trail ride parade, attended a rodeo, toured the world famous Boys Town, Omaha's Old Market and StratCom. They also attended the Pacific Football game in Lincoln. The crew ate at different locations including the VIP cookout at Aksarben. Visits to various schools all over Nebraska would become a tradition.

By the end of 2004, the Big Red Sub Club had sponsored 28 crew visits to the state involving nearly 200 of *Nebraska's* sailors. Each year since 1992, four to ten crewmembers come to Nebraska twice-a-year. Their transportation to the state and during the visit, meals, tours and lodging are paid for by the club and various individuals. The Nebraska Admirals Association continues to be a vital supporter of the visits and other activities as well. The honored visitors have extensively toured the Cornhusker State. Some of the tours have included, the Desoto Bend National Refuge & Museum, Freedom Park, the Strategic Air & Space Museum, State Capitol, cruises on the Missouri River, Homestead National Monument, Fort Atkinson State Park, Arbor Lodge and American Gramaphone Records in the eastern part of the state. In the central part of the state they've enjoyed tours of the Nebraska Law Enforcement Training Center, the Hastings Museum of Natural & Cultural History, program and tour of Naval Ammunition Depot-Hastings State Historic Site, Pioneer Village, Great Platte River Road Archway Monument and in the western part of the state have been special guests at NebraskaLand Days, Buffalo Bill's Scout's Rest Ranch and the Adams Land & Cattle Company.

USS Nebraska crew members tour U.S. Naval Ammunition Depot
State Historic Site at Hastings, NE during a visit in September, 2004.
(Author's photo)

A number of hosts have sponsored a variety of dining experiences for the crews ranging from the Omaha Press Club, steak houses, cookouts at Freedom Park and the Lake Manawa Sailing Club, to dinners at Legion Clubs, and a bar and grill full of mounted wild animals. Many BRSC and NAA members have had the sailors as dinner guests in their own homes. On many occasions throughout the state, individuals will provide rooms in their homes for the men to stay. After the visits, crewmen often write to the BRSC to express their gratitude. Comments like these are not uncommon, "Knowing that people like you and the citizens of Nebraska support us, makes it easier to go out on patrol to do my job…Thank you for taking time out to show us how your state lives from day to day, and what wonderful people they are, I am very grateful…It is a wonderful morale boost to go to a place where my work and sacrifices are appreciated so much."

Each March a USS *Nebraska* commander and his wife are special guests at the Nebraska Statehood Day banquet in Lincoln. Occasionally, sailors return to the state to be present at a particular ceremony as on March 27, 2000, for the 2nd Day Issue Ceremony of the postal stamps honoring 100 years of U.S. Navy submarines.

The Nebraska Press Association (NPA) has been, and continues to be, another leading force in the support of the *Nebraska* and its crew. Past Nebraska Secretary of State, and current Executive Director of the NPA, Allen Beermann, has been a highly visible member of the support since the beginning. One of the original committee members, and a BRSC member, Beermann helps organize and supervise crew visits and trips for Nebraskans to see the submarine. Ever the diplomat, he is adept at speaking in honor of the officers and crew, and welcoming them during these visits. Visiting *Nebraska* crewmembers have been interviewed by radio, television and newspaper media across the state.

The USS *Nebraska* drew national attention in 2001 after a book was written about her. During the late 1990s, Commander Dave Volonino (Blue) had a ride along. *Time* magazine correspondent Douglas C. Waller was writing a book about the *Nebraska*, the crew and the jobs of Trident submariners. He spent weeks at sea visiting, interviewing and sharing the experience of a busy crew. Waller had written *The Commandos: The Inside Story of America's Secret Soldiers* and *Air Warriors: The Inside Story of the Making of a Navy Pilot* and was well-received by the military. This notoriety went nowhere when it came to the secretive submarine service. After making numerous contacts he finally received approval to sail with the *Nebraska*. The result of his work culminated with the aptly titled book *Big Red—Three Months On Board a Trident Nuclear Submarine* (2001). Originally released in hardcover, *Big Red* also has been available in audio book (2001), mass market paperback (2002), and trade paperback (2004) editions. On March 2,

2001, former *Nebraska* commander, Captain Dave Volonino and his COB, Dave Weller returned to the state to sign the books with author Douglas Waller, at the Barnes & Noble Crossroads store in Omaha.

Commander Volonino also hosted a film crew from the Discovery Channel. He was interviewed and the *Nebraska* was featured on the cable television program called "Extreme Machines Military Force: Sea Power," which also was made available in a Discovery Channel Video. The program featured surface ships, attack submarines and the Trident missile submarine.

The mystique of "Big Red" pride appears to be somewhat unique. During the visit to Naval Base Kitsap (NBK) for the Change of Port ceremony in October 2004, sailors were heard to comment on the state support the *Nebraska* receives. Most of the other Trident submarine's crews participate in visits at one time or another to their namesake state, but one would be hard-pressed to find the level of organized support found in the Cornhusker State. It has been noticed by commanders of other boats as well.

During banquets at NBK, Commander John Carter, new Blue Crew commander of the *Nebraska*, told the group, "I am truly impressed by the warmth and the welcome from the State of Nebraska folks, who apparently have a really close relationship with the ship and I'm happy to be a part of that…not all ships have the benefit of having such a strong support in either their name city or their name state."

When Submarine Group Nine Commander, Admiral Melvin Williams spoke, he explained that when he commanded the *Nebraska* he noticed the crew "… elected to go out on liberty wearing "Nebraska wear," with the big red N." On one occasion, when a certain national football championship between Nebraska and a "southeastern state" was about to be played, the COB told the sailors that they may not want to wear the "Nebraska wear" while on liberty in Jacksonville (FL), but they chose to wear it anyway, demonstrating to the COB and Williams the level of pride they had for their boat and namesake state.

Commander Christian Haugen spoke about his last tour as captain of Big Red, and told the group, "After the trips I've made to Nebraska and the 10th anniversary celebration at Kings Bay, I'm overwhelmed by the good will and the gratitude and appreciation you show for the work of submarines and submariners, as that embodied in your ship, *Nebraska*. My men are not fully enumerated for the talent they possess and skills they bring to bear and the hours and dedication they bring to their job. What you bring when you come out there (to the ship) goes a long way in providing job satisfaction that keeps them coming back and makes what they do meaningful and worthwhile, and I'm very grateful for that."

Oh yes, there's a lot more to "Big Red" pride than meets the eye. It's difficult to explain the phenomenon that is so widespread, so emotional and so contagious. Patriotism is a major part, no doubt. But, it goes further than that, as one commander believed when he said, "You folks *really care*."

Senator J. James Exon summed it up well at the *Nebraska's* commissioning in 1993, "So, as we commission this ship named after the great state of Nebraska, let me reiterate, as I did at her christening, the everlasting bond between this ship and crews and the people of our state, as you prowl the depths, always take with you our great Nebraska spirit. As you serve the nation, so we will serve and support you in any way possible."[2]

Chapter 8

Nebraska Name Related Ships

Among the highest honors the Navy can bestow is to name a newly built ship after an officer or enlisted man who gallantly gave his life in combat. Represented here is a selection of U.S. Navy vessels specifically named for cities, counties, rivers and heroic sailors of Nebraska. The Department of the Navy's Naval Historical Center (Navy Yard, Washington, D.C.) was the primary source of information for these ships. This is not intended to be an all-inclusive list, but one that highlights a majority of the subjects. Several vessels that had shared names, for example the USS *Deuel*, named for counties in Nebraska and South Dakota, and USS *Fillmore*, named for counties in Nebraska and Minnesota, were omitted. Some shared names between several counties. This isn't meant to denigrate those with shared names which continue to be a source of pride for citizens and veterans alike. Just one example of this pride is shown by the memorial located inside the Deuel County (NE) courthouse which honors the USS *Deuel*. For this work however, I chose to cover only those with Nebraska-specific names.

The number of United States Naval vessels that have carried Nebraska-related names is generally unknown to the public. This chapter will provide a look at some of their interesting histories. The ships depicted here are listed in alphabetical order according to official Navy lists.

USS *Banner* APA-60
Named for a county in Nebraska.
(*Gillam* class attack transport)

Displacement: 4,247 tons Length: 426' Width: 58' Draft: 16' Crew: 320

The first *Banner* was built in 1944, by the Consolidated Steel Corp. Ltd., of Wilmington, California. The ship was sponsored by Miss Grace Henley and was commissioned September 16, 1944. She reported to the Pacific Fleet under command of Lieutenant Commander J. R. Pace, USN.

The *Banner* carried cargo and troops to Milne Bay, New Guinea, in November 1944. She continued to transport troops between Humboldt Bay, Hollandia, and Cape Sansapor, New Guinea, through December. The next trip was from New Guinea to Luzon, Philippine Islands (P.I.), unloading supplies January 9, 1945. She arrived at Leyte, P.I. on January 14, and then sailed to the Admiralty Islands on the 24th.

A capacity load of troops and cargo was carried to Okinawa on the April 1. On April 5, she departed for San Francisco to pick up troops headed for Leyte, P.I. She would carry more troops to the P.I. area before starting to return them to the U.S. in September 1945.

She continued transport duty through the first of the year until being assigned as a target vessel in February 1946. Later that year, *Banner* was used as a target ship during atomic bomb tests at Bikini Atoll.

She was decommissioned August 27, 1946, and scuttled off Kwajalein in February 1948. The *Banner* received two battle stars for her service during World War II.

USS *Banner* AKL-25 (Later AGER-1)
Named for a county in Nebraska.
(*Camano* class light auxiliary cargo ship)

Displacement: 550 tons Length: 177' Width: 33' Draft: 10' Crew: 40

The second *Banner* was built by the Kewaukee Shipbuilding and Engineering Corp., of Kewaukee, Wisconsin, for the Army as FS-345 and was transferred to the Navy July 1, 1950. She was commissioned on November 24, 1952, with Lieutenant H.W. Atkisson, USN, in command. The ship was assigned to the Service Division 51, Pacific Fleet. She transported supplies including, diesel fuel, ammunition and troops all over the Pacific Ocean.

The success of the Soviet Union's intelligence-gathering "fishing trawlers" prompted the U.S. to look at its program. The Navy already had a series of converted WWII liberty ships for intelligence duties that were successful, but costly to operate. Many believed that it was worth experimenting with smaller, less-offensive-appearing and more economical ships. A plan was approved and implemented by a joint operation of the U.S. Navy and the National Security Agency (NSA). The first ship chosen for conversion to Auxiliary General Environmental

Research (AGER) vessel was the USS *Banner* AKL-25, which was re-designated AGER-1.

The *Banner* successfully carried out intelligence-gathering operations off the coasts of the Soviet Union, China and North Korea in 1967. Subsequently, two more AKL's were converted, the USS *Pueblo* AGER-2 (later famous when the North Koreans seized the ship and held its 82 crewmembers for 11 months) and the USS *Palm Beach* AGER-3. The *Pueblo* served in the western Pacific with the *Banner* and the *Palm Beach* went to the Atlantic Ocean.

USS *Bruce* DD-329
Named for Grand Island, Nebraska native LT Frank Bruce, USN.
(*Clemson* class destroyer)

Displacement: 1,215 tons Length: 314' Width: 31' Draft: 9' Crew: 122

Frank Bruce was born August 20, 1870, in Grand Island, Nebraska. In 1911 he joined the U.S. Navy as a warrant boatswain and temporarily as lieutenant in 1918. He was given command of the minesweeper USS *Bobolink* AMS-20. During World War I, more than 70,000 mines were laid as defense against German submarines. Retrieval of these mines was dangerous work. On May 17, 1919, one such mine exploded, killing Lieutenant Bruce.

The USS *Bruce* was built by the Bethlehem Shipbuilding Corp. of San Francisco. Annie Bruce, the lieutenant's widow, christened the ship when it was launched May 20, 1920. Lieutenant Commander G. N. Reeves, Jr. USN, served as commanding officer when the ship was commissioned September 20 of that year. One of the 150 strong *Clemson* class, the destroyer was armed with four, four-inch and one, three-inch guns, plus 12 torpedo tubes.

Bruce was assigned to the Pacific Fleet at San Diego and took part in engineering, gunnery and torpedo training exercises. She was transferred to Boston in 1921 to become part of Destroyer Division 27, Scouting Fleet. In December 1924, her commander also became Division 27 commander. She again was transferred, this time to the Norfolk Navy Yard in 1925. She served with U.S. Naval Forces—Europe during 1926 and in Cuban waters the following year. For the next few years, she served along the Atlantic coast until docking at the Philadelphia Navy Yard in September 1929.

On May 1, 1930, four months short of ten years' service, USS *Bruce* was decommissioned. She was towed to the Norfolk Navy Yard for experimental strength tests before being scrapped (in accordance with the London Arms Reduction Treaty) in 1932.

USS *Calamus* AOG-25
Named for a river in Nebraska.
(*Mattawee* class gasoline tanker)

Displacement: 845 tons Length: 220' Width: 37' Draft: 13' Crew: 62

The *Calamus* was built by the East Coast Shipyard, Inc., of Bayonne, N.J. The tanker was sponsored by Mrs. A. H. Moore and commissioned July 7, 1944, with Lieutenant W. Hord, commanding. In September 1944, *Calamus* sailed from the Norfolk Navy Yard to Pearl Harbor, Hawaii, to commence station tanker duties. During January and February 1945, she was stationed at Eniwetok to refuel those ships preparing for the attack on Iwo Jima. During service at Saipan and Okinawa, she endured constant Japanese air attacks. *Calamus* returned to San Francisco on March 20, 1946 and was decommissioned May 15, 1946 after earning one battle star for her WWII service.

USS *Chadron* PC-564
Named for a city in Nebraska.
(*PC-461* class patrol craft)

Displacement: 280 tons Length: 175' Width: 23' Draft: 10' Crew: 59

The *Chadron* was built by the Consolidated Shipbuilding Company, of Bronx, NY. She was launched April 12, 1942, and commissioned *PC-564* July 2. She was equipped with one, three-inch gun, one 40mm gun, three 20mm guns, two rocket launchers, two depth charge racks and was powered by two Fairbanks Morse 38D8 1/8 diesel engines. The craft was capable of twenty knots.

In March 1945, the *PC-564* engaged four German minesweepers and nine smaller craft off the coast of Chaussey, France. She managed to outrun the group and ran aground on the French coast at Pierre de Herpin light. Presuming the damage would cause her to sink, 15 crewmen abandoned ship, 14 of which were captured by the enemy. French fishing boats helped the remaining crew and towed the patrol boat into St. Malo Harbor. It was later decommissioned and laid up in the reserve fleet.

She was renamed USS *Chadron* PC-564 February 15, 1956, and transferred to South Korea in 1964. It was then renamed *Sol Ak* (PC-709). She was decommissioned and struck from the Naval Register January 12, 1974.

USS *Collett* DD-730

Named after Omaha native LTCMDR John Austin Collett, USN.

(*Allen M. Sumner* class destroyer)

Displacement: 2,200 tons Length: 376' Width: 41' Draft: 19' Crew: 336

John Austin Collett was born March 31, 1908, in Omaha, Nebraska. He graduated from the U.S. Naval Academy in 1929. While commanding Torpedo Squadron 10, *Enterprise* CV-6, he was killed in action during the Battle of the Santa Cruz Islands October 26, 1942.

USS *Collett* DD-730 was built by Bath Iron Works Corporation of Bath, Maine and launched on March 5, 1944. Mrs. C. C. Baughman was sponsor by proxy for Mrs. J. D. Collett. The ship was commissioned May 16, 1944, with Commander J. D. Collett in command.

Collett operated with the Pacific Fleet and from Ulithi she screened the large task force TF 38 for the remainder of World War II. She saw action in air raids on Luzon and Formosa, which accompanied invasion of ground forces on Leyte. In January 1945, the carriers of her task force launched air attacks on Formosa, the China coast and the Nansei Shoto. On February 16–17, *Collett* went into even more dangerous waters close to the Japanese coast to shell targets on Honshu before giving air cover for the Iwo Jima invasion.

She returned to the Japanese coast with the carrier force and screened them while launching air strikes against Honshu and Okino Daito Shima. On April 18, *Collett* assisted four other destroyers and carrier aircraft in sinking Japanese submarine *I-56*.

After a re-supply stop at Ulithi, she rejoined the task force during the last heavy air attacks on the Japanese homeland. Deploying with her squadron, they sank several merchantmen at Sagami Nada July 22–23. *Collett* entered Tokyo Bay September 14, 1945. A few days later she returned to the West Coast for an overhaul.

The USS *Collett* continued to serve tours of duty in the Far East and was at her station when the Korean War began in June 1950. She patrolled off Pusan from her base at Sasebo, Japan and escorted cargo ships up the channel to Inchon September 13, where she conducted a pre-invasion bombardment. During this action, she was hit four times, wounding five of her crewmen. On the 15th *Collett* returned with an invasion force and provided fire support for the landings. Her outstanding service at Inchon was recognized with a Navy Unit Commendation.

Her second tour of duty in the Korean War lasted from June 1951 to February 1952. She screened TF 77 and conducted shore bombardments along the Korean coast. Her third tour, similar in nature, lasted from August 1952 to April 1953.

The USS *Collett* continued to serve in the Far East through the rest of the 1950s. During the first six months of 1960, she underwent extensive modernization. On July 19, 1960, she collided with *Ammen* DD-527 off the California coast near Long Beach. Eleven members of *Ammen's* crew were killed and twenty were injured. *Collett* suffered a badly damaged bow but was able to make it into port at the Long Beach Naval Shipyard. The entire bow was removed from an uncompleted destroyer in the Reserve Fleet and used to replace the damaged area.

The USS *Collett* received six battle stars for World War II service, the Navy Unit Commendation, and six battle stars for her service during the Korean War.

USS Collett (DD-730), an Allen M. Sumner class destroyer, named after Omaha, NE native John Austin Collett. (U.S. Naval Historical Center)

USS *Don O. Woods* DE-721 (& APD-118)
Named for Kearney, Nebraska native Hospital Apprentice 1ˢᵗ Class Don Otis Woods.
(*Crosley* class high speed transport)

Displacment: 1,450 tons Length: 306' Width: 36' Draft: 13' Crew: 266

Don O. Woods was born in Kearney, Nebraska May 19, 1922, and grew up in Wymore. He enlisted in the Navy June 12, 1940. By 1942, Woods was a Hospital Apprentice First Class assigned to the 1ˢᵗ Marine Division. During the assault on the Gavutu, Solomon Islands, he continued to give medical aid to wounded Marines under fire from Japanese snipers, until he was killed. He was posthumously awarded the Silver Star "for conspicuous gallantry and intrepid conduct under fire."

The *Don O. Woods* was built by the Dravo Corporation, at Neville Island, Pittsburgh, Pennsylvania. It was sponsored by Mrs. H. R. Woods, mother of Hospital Apprentice First Class Woods. Launched as DE-721 (destroyer escort), she was reclassified as APD-118 July 17, 1944, and floated to the Consolidated Shipbuilding Co., of Orange, Texas, for completion as a high-speed transport. The guns were retained but a large deckhouse was constructed to house 160 troops and landing craft. The ship was commissioned May 28, 1945, with Lieutenant Commander L. H. Crosby, USNR, in command.

Assigned to the Pacific Fleet, she left Norfolk Naval Yard and was transiting the Panama Canal when the Japanese surrendered August 9, 1945. After stopping at San Diego, she arrived at Pearl Harbor September 7. The ship transported Army and Navy personnel to Saipan, then went on to Leyte, P.I., arriving October 7, 1945. She served in the Philippines until arriving at San Pedro, California, February 13, 1946. She was decommissioned June 18. The USS *Don O. Woods* was struck from the Naval Register December 12, 1963, and sold to the Republic of Mexico. She serves in the Mexican Navy as the *Usumacinta*.

USS *Elkhorn* AOG-7
Named for a river in Nebraska.
(*Patapsco* class gasoline tanker)

Displacement: 1,850 tons Length: 310' Width: 48' Draft: 13' Crew: 131

Elkhorn was built by Cargill, Inc., at Savage, Minnesota. She was commissioned February 12, 1944, sponsored by Mrs. J. A. Flynn with Lieutenant Junior Grade T. A. Norris, USNR, in command. She arrived at Milne Bay, New Guinea,

May 29, 1944, for station tanker duty, serving in this area until March 1945. The rest of the year was spent on station in the Philippines until she was sent to the west coast for overhaul.

Elkhorn continued to serve the Pacific Fleet, out of Pearl Harbor through 1962, which included the Korean theatre of war. During 1956–57, she carried out arctic re-supply missions to Icy Cape and Point Barrow.

USS *Gage* APA-168
Named for a county in Nebraska.
(*Haskell* class attack transport)

Displacement: 6,720 tons Length: 455' Width: 62' Draft: 24' Crew: 692

Gage was built by the Oregon Shipbuilding Corporation in Portland, Oregon, and launched October 14, 1944, with Mrs. H. L. Edmunds sponsoring. The *Gage* was commissioned November 12, 1944, with Commander L. J. Alexanderson, USNR, commanding.

In January 1945, she sailed for the South Pacific. By February 4, she had delivered nearly 300 marines and equipment to Guadalcanal, a staging area for the assault on Okinawa, and then took part in the attack. During five days of ferocious battle, the *Gage* landed marines of the 3rd Battalion, 4th Regiment, 6th Division, a Navy SeaBee battalion, a medical company and tons of combat equipment.

She returned to San Francisco in May 1945, where she loaded men and equipment of the Army Air Corps and landed them at Manila, Luzon, P.I., on June 12, 1945. She joined Amphibious Group 9 at Leyte June 22, before returning again to San Francisco for repairs. She was in Todd's Drydock at Seattle, Washington, when the Japanese surrendered.

In late August she transported 1,700 Army replacements to Saipan, where she loaded 1,500 marines bound for Japan to serve as occupation forces. Several more trips were made from the western Pacific to the U.S. and back, transporting fresh troops and returning veterans. Leaving Sasebo, Japan June 26, 1946, she returned troops to Hawaii before sailing to Norfolk Navy Yard via the Panama Canal.

She was decommissioned at Norfolk February 26, 1947, and was placed in the Atlantic Reserve Fleet until her name was struck from the Navy list October 1, 1958. She was transferred to the Maritime Commission Reserve Fleet and presently is docked in the James River near Ft. Eustis, Virginia. *Gage* received one battle star for her WWII service.

The USS *Gage*, the only surviving attack transport in its original wartime configuration (out of 230 APAs), is a subject of the APA Historical Preservation Project. The Project is a nonprofit organization dedicated to preserving the history of attack transports and amphibious operations of World War II, Korea and Vietnam. The Project is trying to raise funds to acquire and restore the *Gage*, which was slated for disposal in the fall of 2004. Fortunately, in April 2004, the scheduled disposal was cancelled pending a historic assessment review.

USS *Gosper* APA-170
Named for a county in Nebraska.
(*Haskell* class attack transport)

Displacement: 6,720 tons Length: 455' Width: 62' Draft: 24' Crew: 692

Gosper also was built by the Oregon Shipbuilding Corp., and was launched October 20, 1944, with Mrs. E. P. Nelson, sponsoring. The *Gosper* was commissioned November 18, 1944, under command of Commander F. W. McCann, USN.

Gosper transported troops and supplies to Pearl Harbor during January and February 1945. At Pearl, she was converted into a casualty evacuation transport and was equipped with operating rooms and other necessary hospital facilities. She took part in the invasion of Okinawa in April and was under constant attack by Japanese suicide planes which sunk the USS *Hobbs Victory, Logan Victory* and *LST-447*. The *Gosper* shot down at least one enemy plane. She continued her troop transportation and hospital service in the South Pacific and later returned to San Francisco as part of a convoy. She was undergoing repairs from the heated battle when the war ended.

After resuming her service, she transported occupation troops to the Far East. Anchoring at Manila, P.I., September 15, 1945, she embarked a large group of U.S., British and Canadian servicemen who had been prisoners-of-war since 1941. She moved the troops via Pearl Harbor to Seattle, Washington and continued returning more troops to the mainland.

Gosper departed the Pacific Theatre February 8, 1946, and traveling through the Panama Canal, arrived at Newport News, Virginia, on the 24th. USS *Gosper* was decommissioned April 10, 1946 and was placed in the National Defense Reserve Fleet in the James River. She received one battle star for her WWII service.

USS *Grand Island* PF-14
Named for a city in Nebraska.
(*Tacoma* class patrol frigate)

Displacement: 1,430 tons Length: 304' Width: 38' Draft: 12' Crew: 215

Grand Island was built by Kaiser Cargo, Inc., of Richmond, California, and was launched February 19, 1944, sponsored by Mrs. William Shackleton. She was commissioned May 27, 1944, with Lieutenant Commander H. L. Morgan, USN, commanding.

These ships utilized the British *River* design despite carrying heavier armament than their counterparts. Of the original class of 100, 21 of these were turned over to the Royal Navy under the Lend-Lease program, and the construction contracts of four were cancelled.

On September 12, 1944, *Grand Island* was assigned to the 12th Naval District on the West Coast. She was one of 75 patrol frigates crewed by members of the U.S. Coast Guard, because during wartime, the Coast Guard becomes part of the Navy. She performed weather station and plane guard duty out of San Francisco as well as training exercises with patrol forces. In addition to patrol, she conducted anti-submarine escort duty.

On March 26, 1946, she left San Francisco, traversed the Panama Canal, and arrived at Charleston, South Carolina April 13. The *Grand Island* decommissioned May 21, 1946, and was stricken from the Navy Register. She subsequently was turned over to the State Department Foreign Liquidation Corporation and transferred to Cuba on June 16, 1947. The Cuban government changed the name to *Maximo Gomez*.

In the late 1990s, an Illinois native who served on the *Grand Island* visited her namesake city on a trip west. John Thornbloom, a Coast Guard veteran, stopped at the Grand Island City Hall to give thanks to the citizens who during the war had donated a radio/record player for the ship. He said it helped the crew feel like they were closer to home. While at city hall, Thornbloom was able to see a special display in the Community Room that is dedicated to the USS *Grand Island* and both the USS *Nebraska* battleship and submarine. A 48-star flag, used at the launching of the battleship, is a special feature of the display.[1]

The Tacoma class patrol frigate USS Grand Island (PF-14) was named for the central Nebraska city of Grand Island. (U.S. Navy)

USS *Hurst* DE-250
Named for Falls City, Nebraska native LT Edwin William Hurst, USN.
(*Edsall* class destroyer escort)

Displacement: 1,200 tons Length: 306' Width: 36' Draft: 8' Crew: 186

Edwin W. Hurst was born in Falls City, Nebraska, October 16, 1910, and graduated from the U.S. Naval Academy in June 1932. After serving on the USS *Tennessee* BB-43, he completed flight training in 1935. Following several different squadron assignments, he became a member of the USS *Lexington's* Torpedo Squadron 2, May 19, 1941. During the Battle of Coral Sea in May 1942, Hurst attacked the Japanese carrier *Shoho*, contributing to her sinking, and the carrier *Shokaku* severely damaging her. He was also credited with successfully attacking enemy shipping and shore installations at Salamaua and Lae, New Guinea March 10, 1942, and was awarded the Distinguished Flying Cross for his heroic conduct. He also received the Navy Cross for his service as executive officer of Torpedo Squadron 2. During the ferocious Battle of Coral Sea, the *Lexington* was sunk, and Hurst subsequently flew from New Zealand. He was killed June 9, 1942, when his plane crashed near a Royal New Zealand Air Force Base.

The USS *Hurst* was built by the Brown Shipbuilding Company at Houston, Texas. She was launched April 14, 1943, and sponsored by Mrs. Jeanette Harris Hurst, Lieutenant Hurst's widow. The destroyer escort was commissioned August 30, 1943, with Lieutenant Commander B. H. Brallier commanding. After a brief period of outfitting and shakedown, she returned to Charleston before joining Escort Division 20 at Norfolk in November. Her first convoy duty began December 14, 1943, which took her to Casablanca, and then to New York January 24, 1944. She participated in gunnery and antisubmarine warfare exercises in Casco Bay, Maine, before leaving for another convoy mission on February 23. The USS *Hurst* arrived at Lisahally, Northern Ireland, March 5, 1944 and later returned to New York with another convoy.

After completing 13 convoy escort voyages, most of which were from Boston or New York, to Northern Ireland and England, the *Hurst* was transferred to the Pacific Fleet, arriving at Pearl Harbor July 26, 1945. After World War II ended, the ship arrived at Pago Pago and spent the next several weeks searching the islands of Samoa, Fiji and Society, for missing allied troops and remaining Japanese units. She completed these duties November 3, and headed for San Diego via Pearl Harbor. She arrived in New York harbor December 10 and ultimately sailed to Green Cove Springs, Florida, where she was decommissioned May 1, 1946. In January 1947, the *Hurst* was transferred to the reserve fleet at Orange, Texas.

On January 1, 1973, *Hurst* was transferred to the Mexican navy and was renamed *Manuel Azueta* E-30, and was in service as a training ship as of 2000.

USS *Kirkpatrick* DE-318 (& DER-318)
Named for Cozad, Nebraska native CAPT Thomas L. Kirkpatrick, USN.
(*Edsall* class destroyer escort)

Displacement: 1,200 tons Length: 306' Width: 36' Draft: 8' Crew: 186

Thomas L. Kirkpatrick was born in Cozad, Nebraska, on July 5, 1887. He was appointed acting Chaplain, U.S. Navy February 19, 1918 serving stations in the United States and abroad. He was assigned to the USS *North Dakota* BB-29 June 24, 1919. For the next 20 years he completed assignments on the *Utah*, *Pittsburgh* and *Saratoga* and at Samoa from 1935 to 1937. He reported to his final assignment September 13, 1940, which was aboard the battleship *Arizona* BB-39, September 13, 1940. In July 1941, Kirkpatrick was commissioned Captain (Chaplain Corps). On Sunday morning, December 7, 1941, Captain Kirkpatrick was in the wardroom enjoying a cup of coffee with fellow officers. According to the National Park Service—*Arizona* Memorial, when General Quarters sounded, Kirkpatrick rushed to sickbay, which was his battle station. Sickbay was located just forward of turret number 1, on the second deck. He was killed in the massive explosions of the forward magazines when the Japanese attacked.

The *Kirkpatrick* was built by the Consolidated Steel Corporation in Orange, Texas. Launched June 5, 1943, the destroyer escort was sponsored by Captain Kirkpatrick's widow, Genevieve. The ship was commissioned October 23, 1943, with Lieutenant Commander V. E. Bakanas, U.S. Coast Guard, in command.

After reporting to Norfolk Naval Base December 23, she began transatlantic escort duty. She made one escort crossing to the Mediterranean, and 10 to the British Isles between January 1944 and May 1945. During her third voyage, April 16, 1944, another escort in the convoy, USS *Gaudy* DE-764, rammed German submarine *U-550* after the U-boat sunk a tanker in the convoy. Eleven enemy sailors were captured.

The *Kirkpatrick* was transferred to the Pacific Fleet after victory in Europe was achieved and arrived at Pearl Harbor July 11, 1945. She performed additional escort duties until arriving back at Charleston Navy Yard December 8. She was decommissioned on May 1, 1946, at Green Cove Springs, Florida.

The ship was reclassified as a radar picket ship DER-318, October 1, 1951 and recommissioned February 23, 1952, with Lieutenant Commander George S. Davis in command. She served radar picket operations in the Atlantic Barrier, the seaward extension of the Distant Early Warning (DEW), line across northern Canada. The ship served in this capacity and also visited northern European ports until 1960. The USS *Kirkpatrick* was decommissioned March 29, 1960, at the Philadelphia Naval Yard and entered the Atlantic Reserve Fleet.

The USS Kirkpatrick (DE-318) was named for Cozad, NE native Captain Thomas L. Kirkpatrick. who was killed aboard the USS Arizona December 7, 1941. (U.S. Navy)

USS *Kyne* DE-744
Named for Ringgold, Nebraska native ENS Elden Francis Kyne, USN
(*Cannon* class destroyer escort)

Displacement: 1,240 tons Length: 306' Width: 36' Draft: 8' Crew: 186

Elden F. Kyne was born in Ringgold, Nebraska, June 4, 1910. He enlisted in the U.S. Navy February 1, 1929 and appointed Machinist April 15, 1941. He was assigned to the USS *Astoria* CA-34 (Heavy Cruiser) August 8, of that year. Kyne was commissioned Ensign June 15, 1942. During the battle of Savo Island, Ensign Kyne was killed in action when Japanese naval forces sunk the *Astoria*.

The USS *Kyne* was built by the Western Pipe & Steel Company at Los Angeles, California. She was launched August 15, 1943, and was sponsored by Kyne's widow, Alma. The ship was commissioned April 4, 1944, with Commander A. Jackson, Jr., in command.

Kyne left the West Coast June 6, 1944, to join the Pacific Fleet. She screened task forces supporting the invasions of the Palau Islands, and escorted convoys transporting wounded Marines from battle. She continued the escort and support of operations in Ulithi, the Philippines, Iwo Jima, and Borneo.

The ship arrived in Tokyo Bay August 28, 1945, as part of occupation forces. She left Yokosuka on October 2, and arrived at Philadelphia November 23rd. The USS *Kyne* was decommissioned June 14, 1946, at Green Cove Springs, Florida.

Her service not yet over, she was designated in service and operated as a training ship from Fort Schuyler, New York, until being recommissioned November 21, 1950, with Lieutenant Commander Carl L. Scherrer commanding. She was assigned to the 3rd Naval District for the next nine years as a training ship. The *Kyne* was decommissioned for a second time June 17, 1960, at New York, and placed in the Atlantic Reserve Fleet. She received six battle stars for World War II service.

USS *Marts* DE-174
Named for Wilsonville, Nebraska native Fireman 2nd Class Alvin Lee Marts
(*Cannon* class destroyer escort)

Displacement: 1,240 tons Length: 306' Width: 36' Draft: 8' Crew: 186

Alvin Lee Marts was born at Wilsonville, Nebraska, August 4, 1923. On July 2, 1941, he enlisted in the Navy at Denver, Colorado. He served on the carrier *Yorktown* CV-5 until she was sunk at the Battle of Midway. He survived and was transferred to the heavy cruiser *New Orleans* CA-32, as a Fireman 2nd Class. During the battle of the southern Solomon Islands, the cruiser and destroyer force that included *New Orleans* fought Japanese destroyers in Ironbottom Sound November 30, 1942. The *New Orleans* took a torpedo hit to the port side of the bow exploding two magazines. The resulting explosion tore off the forward portion of the ship back to the No. 2 turret. Marts was gravely injured from the blast and fires but in total disregard of his safety, carried an injured medical officer to the battle dressing station amidships. He collapsed and died of his wounds shortly afterwards. For extreme gallantry and self-sacrificing devotion to a stricken comrade, Fireman 2nd Class Marts was posthumously awarded the Navy Cross.

The USS *Marts* was built by the Federal Shipbuilding & Dry Dock Company, at Newark, New Jersey. She was launched August 8, 1943, and sponsored by Miss Betty Marts (sister). The ship was commissioned on September 3, with Lieutenant Carl M. Fellows in command.

Marts departed New York November 4, 1943, and took up convoy escort duty of the Atlantic coast of South America. For the next five months, she operated in the 4th Fleet, escorting ships between Trinidad, B.W.I. and Recife, Brazil. As an escort for the USS *Omaha* CL-4, she left Bahia, Brazil, May 23, 1944, and patrolled the mid-Atlantic in search of German U-Boats. She escorted *Omaha* to Gibraltar in July and returned to Recife on the 23rd. During July and August, *Marts* screened the British cable repair ship SS *Cambria* during communications cable repairs off Brazil. Afterwards she joined Escort Division 24 on hunter-killer patrols in the Atlantic. Operating with *Tripoli* CVE-64, she made four offensive anti-submarine patrols from Recife. She continued escort duties in this area until the end of January 1945.

On February 1, *Marts* joined *Cincinnati* CL-6 at Bahia and escorted the cruiser on patrol in the South Atlantic for 10 days. On March 2, *Marts* arrived at the Brazilian Naval Base at Natal, where she trained Brazilian sailors. Under the Lend-Lease agreement, she was decommissioned March 20, 1945, and recommissioned the same day in the Brazilian Navy as *Bocaina* D-22. She was returned to the United States June 30, 1953, but was transferred permanently to the Brazilian Navy under terms of the Mutual Defense Assistance Program.

USS *McCandless* FF-1084
Named for Endicott, Nebraska native CMDRE Byron McCandless, USN
and his son RADM Bruce McCandless, USN
(*Knox* class frigate)

Displacement: 4,200 tons Length: 438' Width: 47' Draft: 16' Crew: 285

Byron McCandless was born September 5, 1881, at Endicott, Nebraska. By the late 1800s, the family moved to what is now Florence, Colorado (named for Florence McCandless). He attended the Colorado School of Mines and graduated from the U. S. Naval Academy in 1905. McCandless made the historic world-cruise with the "Great White Fleet," and later served as a flag lieutenant and aide to Rear Admiral Charles J. Badger, Commander-in-Chief Atlantic Fleet. From 1915–1917, he was aide to the first Chief of Naval Operations, William S. Benson and to Secretary of the Navy Josephus Daniels. During World War I, he commanded the destroyer *Caldwell* and was awarded the Navy Cross for his convoy and anti-submarine actions against the Germans in the Atlantic. He later served as Executive Officer of the battleship *Kansas* BB-21, commanded Destroyer Division 30 and was aide and Operations Officer for Destroyer Squadrons of the Scouting Fleet.

Commodore McCandless commanded the fleet oiler *Brazos* in 1927–1928. He then attended the Naval War College before serving as Director of Training, Bureau of Navigation. After completing another advanced course at the Naval

War College, he served as Chief of Staff for Destroyers, Battle Force, from 1935 to 1937.

While serving as commanding officer of the Destroyer Base at San Diego, he was placed on the retired list June 30, 1940, but continued on active duty as Commandant of the Naval Repair Base throughout World War II. Because of high achievements in ship repair, training and housing of personnel, and post-war berthing and preservation of ships, experimentation in infra-red rays for signaling ships at night, construction of Fleet Schools, and the development of audio-visual aides for training purposes, McCandless was awarded the Legion of Merit. He also provided facilities for the Armed Guard School, training thousands of men in repairing some 400 ships per month and added five piers and a graving dock. He also invented a rescue device used to salvage small craft that were damaged on invasion beachheads.

Commodore McCandless was again transferred to the retired list September 25, 1946. He passed away May 30, 1967, at Mariposa, California.

As if the amazing naval career of Commodore Byron McCandless wasn't enough, there's more. During World War I, *National Geographic* magazine hailed McCandless as the world's foremost authority on flags. In 1916, a uniform Presidential flag was adopted by President Woodrow Wilson, replacing the two different flags used by the Army and Navy. President Wilson had instructed then Assistant Secretary of the Navy Franklin D. Roosevelt and the Aide to the Secretary of the Navy Commander Byron McCandless, to design the new flag. In March 1945, President Franklin D. Roosevelt had his Naval Aide ask Commodore McCandless for an updated flag design. His designs were submitted after Roosevelt's death but President Truman was able to review them in June. The President asked him to add a circle of 48 stars (representing all states) which he did. President Truman held a news conference October 25, 1945, where he announced an Executive Order which not only made official the new flag, but also the Presidential coat of arms and the "Seal of the President of the United States," all designed by Commodore Byron McCandless. These emblems of the Commander-in-Chief still are in use today.

Lieutenant (later Commodore) Byron McCandless' son Bruce was born August 12, 1911, in Washington, D.C. A 1932 graduate of the Naval Academy, he was serving as Communications Officer on the cruiser *San Francisco* CA-38, at Pearl Harbor when the Japanese attacked. He continued to serve on the cruiser (which was Admiral Callaghan's flagship) in Pacific island action. During the night of November 13–14, 1942, their task force intercepted a Japanese battle group near Guadalcanal. The *San Francisco* made several devastating hits on two enemy battleships before she was fired upon from three directions. Direct hits to both the navigating bridge and flag-bridge killed Admiral Callaghan and all of his staff except Lieutenant Commander McCandless. Though seriously wounded, he continued to direct his ship's fire until the task force was victorious. McCandless received the Medal of Honor for his supreme courage and leadership that resulted in winning the fierce battle.

In March 1944, he took command of the destroyer *Gregory* and operated off Iwo Jima and Okinawa. He received the Silver Star for gallantry while commanding the *Gregory.* The destroyer was badly damaged April 8, 1945, by attacks from four suicide planes, one of which crashed into the ship. He was ordered to take *Gregory* to San Diego where the ship was repaired under the direction of his father, Commodore Byron McCandless.

After the war, Bruce McCandless was promoted to Captain and held various command positions. He was promoted to Rear Admiral on the basis of his combat awards and was placed on the Retired List September 1, 1952. He died at Washington, D.C., January 24, 1968.

The family legacy continued with Admiral Bruce McCandless' son, Captain Bruce McCandless II, USN, (now retired) who is a celebrated Space Shuttle Astronaut. He graduated second in a class of 899 cadets at the U.S. Naval Academy. He is credited with making the first untethered walk in space while serving as a mission specialist on the space shuttle *Challenger* (STS-41B) in February 1984. He also was part of *Discovery's* (STS-31) crew in April 1990.

The USS *McCandless* was built by Avondale Shipyards of Westwego, Louisiana, and was launched March 20, 1971. She was commissioned March 18, 1972.

McCandless served in the Atlantic Fleet in European waters. She was transferred to the Naval Reserve Force December 31, 1991, and redesignated FFT-1084 (training frigate). The ship was decommissioned May 6, 1994, and transferred to the Turkish navy where she serves as TCG *Trakya* F-254.

USS *Merrick* AKA-97 (& LKA-97)
Named for a county in Nebraska.
(*Andromeda* class amphibious cargo ship)

Displacement: 6,761 tons Length: 459' Width: 63' Draft: 24' Crew: 247

Merrick was built by the Federal Shipbuilding and Drydock Company of Kearny, New Jersey, and was launched January 28, 1945, with Mrs. Francis N. Van Riper, sponsoring. She was commissioned on March 31, 1945, with Lieutenant Commander Walter E. Reed, USNR, commanding.

Merrick transported cargo, landing craft and troops in the Marshall Islands and New Hebrides through the end of World War II. She then transported occupation troops from Hawaii and the Philippines to Japan, and returned veterans, including marine war dogs, back to Norfolk, Virginia.

After serving on the East Coast she sailed with a naval group to California where cargo was loaded for operation "Highjump." This was the largest American Antarctic expedition (until 1968) up to that time. On January 13, 1947, the group reached the Bay of Whales, Antarctica, establishing Little America IV, a base for scientific expeditions. Heavy ice conditions became dangerous and *Merrick's* rudder was damaged. The Coast Guard icebreaker *Northwind* WAGB-282 took her in tow but before clearing the ice, the rudder was completely sheared off. She was towed to New Zealand where repairs were made.

On March 22, 1947, *Merrick* sailed for California, experiencing boiler failures and fuel shortages along the way. She was decommissioned at San Francisco June 23, 1947, and placed in the National Defense Reserve Fleet.

Merrick was recommissioned in January 1952 for service during the Korean War, assigned to Japan for transport duties. In October, she returned to California for overhaul and training, before deploying for a second tour from July 3, 1953 to April 22, 1954. She participated in Operation "Big Switch," the post armistice prisoner exchange.

Merrick was assigned to the 7th Fleet in the Western Pacific through 1963, which included two supply missions to the Arctic. That year also marked the ship's first Vietnam War tour in the South China Sea, which continued through 1969. She was reclassified LKA-97 January 1, 1969.

USS *Niobrara* AO-72
Named for a river in Nebraska.
(*Chiwawa* class oiler)

Displacement: 5,708 tons Length: 502' Width: 68' Draft: 30' Crew: 247

Niobrara was built by the Bethlehem Steel Corporation of Sparrows Point, Maryland, and was launched November 28, 1942, with Mrs. Mark O'Dea, sponsoring. She was commissioned March 13, 1943, with Commander Theodore G. Haff, USN, commanding.

She ferried oil from ports in Texas and Aruba, N.W.I. to Mediterranean ports in support of the North Africa and Sicilian invasions.

Niobrara was modified at Norfolk before heading to Pearl Harbor and on to Kwajalein where she fueled transports bound for the June 1944 invasions of the

Marianas. She also fueled ships of Task Force 38 that were attacking the China coast. She continued to serve in the Pacific Theatre, including the Iwo Jima and Okinawa campaigns until the war's end.

She was present in Tokyo Bay August 30, 1945, to witness the Japanese surrender.

The USS *Niobrara* was decommissioned September 24, 1946, and held in reserve at Philadelphia. On February 5, 1951, she was recommissioned, and served three years with the Atlantic Fleet. Decommissioned again November 30, 1954, the ship was recommissioned at San Francisco December 16, 1956, and again served in the Pacific until sailing to Galveston, Texas, where she decommissioned November 12, 1957. She transferred to the Maritime Administration December 5th and joined the National Defense Reserve Fleet at Beaumont.

The USS *Niobrara* received four battle stars for World War II service.

USS *Omaha*
Named for a city in Nebraska.
(*Serapis* class screw sloop)

Displacement: 2,394 tons Length: 250' Width: 38' Draft: 17' Crew: unknown

The first of three *Omahas* was built of live oak at the Philadelphia Navy Yard and launched June 10, 1869 as *Astoria*. The name was changed to *Omaha* August 10th of that year, and commissioned September 12, 1872, with Captain John C. Febiger, USN, commanding. Miss Kitty Marchand, daughter of Commodore Marchand, was the sponsor.

Omaha served on the South and North Atlantic stations from 1873 to 1879. During 1874–75, three different commanding officers served on her, Captain William K. Mayo, Captain Philip C. Johnson and Captain Edward Simpson.

On March 1, 1877, *Omaha* became the squadron flagship of Rear Admiral George H. Preble, South Pacific Squadron. She arrived at Callao, Peru, June 14, where Admiral Preble conferred with the U.S. Minister relative to the seizure of the steamer *Georgia*, which was thereupon released by the Peruvian authorities. She was dry-docked for a refit at Philadelphia Navy Yard from 1880 to 1884.

In late 1887, under command of Captain Thomas O. Selfridge, Jr., *Omaha* approached Nagasaki, Japan. Captain Selfridge decided to hold target practice which was required every quarter. He found a suitable place on the shore that featured a high cliff which, "...would serve as a backstop for all "overs" and "ricochets." Sailors were stationed abreast of the target area to make sure all shells exploded properly. After practice was completed, with a positive report from the observers, *Omaha* proceeded to Nagasaki. Unfortunately, some inhabitants came down from the opposite side of the cliff and found some unexploded shells. One of the men was a worker from a nearby Japanese arsenal and apparently was attempting to show onlookers one of the shells. He accidentally exploded the shell, killing himself and several others. Captain Selfridge explained in his memoir published in 1924, "On learning of the accident I took *Omaha* back to the island, and made such amends as were possible, including the distribution to the families of the injured of about $600, which the officers and crew of the Omaha had contributed." He regretted the incident but felt that they did what they could under the circumstances. He was sadly disappointed in the repercussions however as he said, "...the Commander-in-Chief, through the American Minister could have easily adjusted the matter with local authorities; especially since it was one of those strange pranks of chance where accident follows from the very fact of extra precaution. However, he saw fit to magnify the incident, to detach me from my command of the ship without any hearing, and to order me to Washington."²

Selfridge Jr. may have felt that a naval officer of his standing was worth extra consideration. He was the son of a career naval officer, who graduated from the U.S. Naval Academy at 17 and the head of his class. Selfridge Jr. was born in Massachusetts in 1836 and graduated from the Naval Academy in 1854. At the beginning of the Civil War, he helped to destroy the Norfolk Navy Yard which fell to the rebel forces. He got away with the sloop of war *Cumberland*, saving it also from the enemy. He participated in the capture of Fort Hatteras and was a lieutenant gunnery officer in charge of a battery of forward 9-inch guns on the *Cumberland*. On March 8, 1862, he survived the sinking of his ship by the ironclad CSS *Virginia* during the famous attack on Hampton Roads. The next day, the historic battle between the USS *Monitor* and the *Virginia*, left the *Monitor's* commander, Captain John L. Worden badly wounded. Assistant Secretary of the Navy Gustavus Fox appointed Lieutenant Selfridge commander of the *Monitor* shortly after the battle. Selfridge later commanded the experimental submarine *Alligator* at the Washington Navy Yard. In the fall of 1862, he was assigned to the Mississippi Squadron and commanded the *Cairo* and *Conestoga*, both of which were sunk in battle. He was known as the only naval officer of the Civil War to have had three ships sunk under him. Back to the East Coast before the end of the war, he commanded *Huron* during the attacks on Fort Fisher, Fort Anderson and the capture of Wilmington. Destroyers later were named for Selfridge Jr., and his father.

Captain Frederick V. McNair assumed command of the *Omaha* on January 6, 1888, and was again the squadron flagship, this time under Rear Admiral Ralph Chandler. Chandler died about a year later at Hong Kong, and was succeeded

April 14, 1889, by Rear Admiral George E. Belknap. On September 21ˢᵗ of that year, Captain Bartlett J. Cromwell took over as commander of *Omaha*.

The *Omaha* served on the Asiatic station through 1891 which included protecting American interests in areas of unrest as indicated by the 1888 *Annual Report of the Secretary of the Navy*, "Vessels of the squadron have visited during the year the principal ports on the west coast of Mexico and Central and South America, but on account of political disturbances in the Hawaiian and Samoan Islands and in Peru, almost the entire force on the station has been kept constantly in the waters of those countries for the protection of the lives and property of our citizens."

On February 8, 1890, she landed men to assist with firefighting in the Japanese town of Hodogaya.

The *Omaha* was decommissioned at Mare Island Navy Yard, California, June 16, 1891, and turned over to the Marine Hospital Service. The ship was anchored off San Francisco as a Quarantine Ship for infectious diseases. She served in this capacity until being struck from the Navy Register July 10, 1914. *Omaha* was sold to Smith and Bondrow April 17, 1915, for $14,140.00.

USS *Omaha* CL-4
Named for a city in Nebraska.
(*Omaha* class light cruiser)

Displacement: 7,050 tons Length: 555' Width: 55' Draft: 20' Crew: 458

The second *Omaha* was built by the Todd Shipbuilding Company of Tacoma, Washington, and was launched December 14, 1920, with Miss Louise Bushnell White, sponsoring. She was commissioned February 24, 1923, with Captain David C. Hanrahan, USN, commanding. The *Omaha* was equipped with 10 six-inch and eight three-inch guns as well as numerous smaller pieces. Two seaplanes, positioned on the stern, were launched by catapults.

Assigned to the Atlantic Fleet, her mission was training and she consistently won fleet awards in gunnery and communications. She visited several ports in the Mediterranean and Caribbean stations.

On November 6, 1941, while on neutrality patrol with USS *Somers* DD-381, *Omaha* spotted a vessel acting suspiciously, so it was ordered to heave to. Even though the vessel flew a U.S. flag, *Omaha's* suspicions were confirmed when the crew attempted to scuttle the ship and abandon it. The *Omaha's* crew managed to salvage the freighter and took her to Puerto Rico. It turned out to be the German ship *Odenwald*, carrying a load of rubber, brass and copper for the German military. A classified Navy report published in 1942, and since declassified, revealed that one of the *Odenwald's* 45 crewmen was Helmut Ruge, 2nd Radio Operator on the ship. It was learned that Ruge was actually a member of the Kriegsmarine (German navy, 1939–45) and had been one of the crewmen of the scuttled pocket battleship *Admiral Graf Spee*. He made his way to Japan where he served in the German Embassy in Tokyo, before being ordered back to Germany. He was on his way home when the *Omaha* and *Somers* intercepted the *Odenwald*.

After the U.S. entered the war, *Omaha* patrolled the South Atlantic with orders to stop Nazi blockade runners. On January 4, 1944, with *Jouett* DD-396, she sighted a ship being scuttled and abandoned by its crew. The next day another ship was sighted that was immediately set on fire by its crew. *Omaha* opened fire and shortly afterwards the vessel sank. It was reported that both ships were carrying cargoes of rubber for the Nazi war machine.

In March 1944, she returned to Naples, Italy, which had been one of her ports of call before the war. She assisted in the invasion of southern France and the island of Poquerolles. *Omaha* was present at the surrender of Giens August 23, and a few days later, bombarded targets in the Toulon area. She then returned to patrol duties in the South Atlantic until the end of World War II.

Omaha was decommissioned November 1, 1945, at the Philadelphia Navy Yard and was scrapped in February 1946. She earned one battle star for her WWII service.

All but one of the 10 ships of the *Omaha* class were scrapped in 1946. They represented an original cost of $135,000,000 but would bring about $50,000 each for scrap. They first were stripped of all armament, radar, navigation instruments, control apparatus, and any other usable equipment.

Many past members of naval vessels have organized associations dedicated to the ships on which they served. The September 15, 1988, issue of the *Omaha World Herald* ran a story about two such members of the USS *Omaha* CL-4 Association who were preparing to attend the annual convention to be held in Omaha, Nebraska. One member, from Gretna, Nebraska, who served on the ship during the early 1940s, explained that when he finished training, the assignments were posted. Beside his name was the word "Omaha," which excited him as he thought that he was going home for recruiting duty. When they were read out loud however, it became clear, "USS *Omaha*, Norfolk, Virginia."

The USS Omaha (CL-4) in her port at Naples, Italy 1938. (Author's collection)

In November 1941, the Omaha and Somers (DD-381) captured the German freighter Odenwald in the south Atlantic. The Omaha's crew posed on their prize with the captured ship's flag. (U.S. Naval Historical Center)

USS *Omaha* SSN-692
Named for a city in Nebraska.
(*Los Angeles* class nuclear attack submarine)

Displacement: 5,700 tons Length: 362' Width: 33' Draft: 32' Crew: 110

The third *Omaha* was built by the Electric Boat Division of General Dynamics Corporation, in Groton, Connecticut. The fifth of a class of 62 boats, *Omaha's* keel was laid January 27, 1973. She was launched February 21, 1976, sponsored by Mrs. Roman L. Hruska. Commissioning took place March 11, 1978, with Commander Ted A. Hamilton, USN, in command.

The purpose of the attack submarine is to escort carrier battle groups and to track and attack enemy submarines and surface ships.

The 1990 price of a *Los Angeles* class submarine was $900 million.

Omaha was placed in reserve February 7, 1995. She was decommissioned and struck from the Naval Vessel Register October 5, 1995, and laid up at Bremerton

Navy Yard (Naval Base Kitsap) in Washington. She is scheduled to enter the Nuclear Powered Ship and Submarine Recycling Program on October 1, 2007.

The USS Omaha (SSN-692) was the fifth in a class of 62 Los Angeles class attack submarines. She is shown at launching February 21, 1976.
(General Dynamics Electric Boat)

USS *Parle* DE-708
Named for Omaha native ENS John J. Parle, USNR.
(*Rudderow* class destroyer escort)

Displacement: 1,810 tons Length: 306' Width: 37' Draft: 13' Crew: 221

Born May 26, 1920, in Omaha, Nebraska, John Joseph Parle enlisted in the U.S. Naval Reserve as Apprentice Seaman in January 1942. After completing Midshipman training at Notre Dame University, he was commissioned Ensign, USNR January 28, 1943. After an assignment with the Amphibious Force at Norfolk, Virginia, he was assigned to the Northwest African Amphibious Force and attached to *LST-375* as officer in charge of small boats during the invasion of Sicily, July 9–10, 1943. During the secret approach, an accidentally-ignited smoke pot was about to touch off a boat loaded with high-explosive charges and ammunition, which would have disclosed to the enemy the pending invasion. He unhesitatingly entered the craft, snuffed out some burning fuses and after failing to extinguish the smoke pot, took it in his bare hands and tossed it overboard. He died a week later as a result of inhaled poisonous fumes and smoke. "For valor and courage above and beyond the call of duty, he was awarded the Congressional Medal of Honor." Ensign Parle's heroic self-sacrifice prevented grave damage to the ship and personnel and insured the security of a vital mission. He gallantly gave his life in the service of his country.

The USS *Parle* was built by the Defoe Shipbuilding Company of Bay City, Michigan, and was launched March 25, 1944, sponsored by Mrs. Harry V. Parle, mother of Ensign Parle. She was commissioned July 29, 1944 with Lieutenant Commander James C. Toft, Jr., USNR, commanding.

Parle was assigned to the Atlantic Fleet for convoy duty, completing an Atlantic-Mediterranean voyage before her permanent assignment to Escort Division 60.

After being fitted out for Pacific duty in December, she reported for duty with the 7th Fleet and was assigned to the Philippine Sea Frontier and routed to Leyte. As an escort with Task Unit 94.18.12, she carried out numerous missions between Kossol Roads, Leyte, Lingayen, Subic, New Guniea, Okinawa, Ulithi and Hollandia.

In August 1945, she was with the Amphibious Forces of the Pacific Fleet escorting occupation troops to Korea. By January, she was sent to the Atlantic Reserve Fleet in Florida.

On March 2, 1951, *Parle* was recommissioned and assigned to the Atlantic Fleet out of Norfolk and Nova Scotia. During the first half of 1952, she was engaged in training at Guantanamo Bay, Cuba, and Key West, Florida for Fleet

Sonar School. The latter part of the year was spent in the North Atlantic and Baltic Sea for fleet exercises. She was used for Anti-Submarine Warfare tactics training in the South Atlantic through 1958.

On January 1, 1959, *Parle* was transferred to the control of Commandant, 5th, Naval District as a Naval Reserve Training Ship. Because of world tensions in August 1961, President Kennedy called for partial mobilization of Reserves and *Parle* rejoined the active fleet for one year.

In July 1962, she reverted to inactive status, again as a Reserve Training Ship. She continued to serve in a training status from her port of Chicago into 1970. The USS *Parle*, the *last active World War II era destroyer escort on the Naval Register,* was decommissioned at Norfolk, Virginia, July 1, 1970.

Unfortunately, with the provenance of being named after a Medal of Honor winner and being the last WWII destroyer escort in service, the lamentable decision was made to end the *Parle's* existence by disgracefully using it as a target. After stripping useable equipment, the ship was towed 80 miles off Mayport, Florida and sunk by an aerial attack. Fortunately, there are two WWII destroyer escorts on public display in the U.S.

The USS Parle (DE-708) was named for Omaha, NE native Ensign John
J. Parle. Ensign Parle was posthumously awarded the Medal of Honor.
(U.S. Navy)

Petalesharo YTB-832
Named for Pawnee Indian Chief born in what is now Nebraska.
(*YTB-760* Class Large Harbor Tug)

Displacement: 346 tons Length: 101' Width: 29' Draft: 14' Crew: 12

Petalesharo, a Skidi Pawnee Chief, was born about 1800 in what is now Nebraska. He was noted for saving a young Comanche girl from being sacrificed in 1817. He convinced his father, then Chief of their tribe, to stop the sacrificial killings. President Monroe asked Petalesharo to visit Washington, D.C., in 1820, where he was presented with a silver medal that read, "Bravest of the Brave."

The *Petalesharo* was built by Marinette Marine and launched October 3, 1974. In 1997, the Trident Refit Facility (TRF), at the Naval Submarine Base (NSB), Kings Bay, Georgia, completed a major overhaul on the tug. Over 50,000 man-hours were invested in replacing the tug's navigational system, updating the shore power system, tanks and engines, saving the Navy $800,000 in fleet maintenance funds by doing the work at NSB Kings Bay.

The tug is operated by a crew of enlisted personnel. She features two state-rooms (each with a lavatory), crew's quarters, a galley with an electric range, a 25-cubic foot refrigerator/freezer, water cooler, shower, lavatory and a water closet. She also is equipped with a 2000 GPM fire pump and firefighting equipment.

In July 1999, the *Petalesharo* was placed in inactive reserve at Submarine Squadron 22, La Maddalena, Italy.

USS *Platte* AO-24
Named for a river in Nebraska.
(*Cimarron* class oiler)

Displacement: 25,440 tons Length: 553' Width: 75' Draft: 32' Crew: 276

The *Platte* was built by the Bethlehem Steel Company in Baltimore, Maryland, and launched July 8, 1939, with Mrs. Harold R. Stark sponsoring. Commander P. L. Meadows was the first commanding officer.

Platte fitted out at the Philadelphia Navy Yard and departed Norfolk March 27, 1940, making trips to the oil docks at Houston, Texas, and supporting the fleet operating in the Panama Canal Zone. She replenished the fleet tugs *Capella* and *Navajo* that were towing the huge floating dry-dock *YFD-2* to Pearl Harbor.

By September, she operated out of San Pedro, California, carrying oil, passengers and freight to Pearl Harbor. She was in the port of San Diego by December 7, 1941.

The *Platte* went to sea as part of a convoy headed for Hawaii with the aircraft carrier USS *Enterprise* CV-6, Admiral William F. Halsey's flagship. The convoy's job was to guard the convoy routes for troop and cargo ships reinforcing the Samoan Islands.

The next months were spent refueling task forces in the Coral Sea area. She then rejoined the *Enterprise* and *Yorktown* task forces, refueling them just before the Battle of Midway.

In August, she supported the *Enterprise* and *Saratoga* task forces in the Solomons. After returning to the West Coast, she resumed support of forces in the battles for Guadalcanal and the Solomons.

On April 9, 1943, *Platte* provided support for the campaign to retake the Aleutians from the Japanese, serving as station tanker in Kulak Bay, Adak. She went on to serve with Service Squadron Eight during the fight for the Gilberts and remained at sea for 30 days at a time. She refueled the *Pennsylvania* and six destroyers in the Marshall Islands, the Marianas and Tinian Island. She operated from Eniwetok in support of the occupation of the Palau Islands, the Carolines and Leyte and Samar in the Philippines.

After an overhaul in the U.S., she again provided support for the Mariana campaign as well as Iwo Jima and carrier strikes on Tokyo. About a month after the August 1945 Japanese surrender, *Platte* entered Tokyo Bay as station tanker.

After a return to the U.S., she arrived at Yokohama, Japan, to support occupation forces February 4, 1946. During the next year, the oiler made several trips to Bahrein, Saudi Arabia, to service fleet operations in Japan, Korea, the Philippines, Okinawa and China.

In early 1951, she refueled cruisers and destroyers of the United Nations Escort and Blockade Force off the coast of Korea. She continued runs from Sasebo, Japan to Korea providing vital fuel and aviation gasoline for fast-attack carriers *Boxer*, *Philippine Sea* and *Bon Homme Richard*. By mid-1953, *Platte* began her third tour of duty in Korean waters. She made almost yearly deployments to the western Pacific through 1968, which included serving in the Vietnam War and refueling the *Enterprise* task force off Korea during the *Pueblo* incident.

The USS *Platte* served into 1970, receiving an amazing 11 battle stars for World War II service, six battle stars for Korean War service and 5 battle stars for Vietnam War service. The *Platte* was sold for scrap on May, 14, 1971.

USS *Platte* AO-186
Named for a river in Nebraska.
(*AO-177* class oiler)

Displacement: 11,482 tons Length: 700' Width: 86' Draft: 33' Crew: 223

The second *Platte* was built by Avondale Shipbuilding of New Orleans, Louisiana, launched January 30, 1982. She was commissioned April 16, 1983.

The February 1999 issue of *All Hands*, an official U.S. Navy magazine, told about a deployment to the Mediterranean where the *Platte*, *"accomplished an incredible maritime feat by transferring 500,000 gallons of fuel to eight NATO force ships in just six hours."* The achievement was especially noted because of the language barrier found among the ships. The crew handling the fuel lines improvised, by using hand signals. Boatswains Mate 2nd Class Edward Klimek, of Grand Island, Nebraska, said, "It was exciting to refuel foreign ships...we had no choice but to find a different way to communicate with them."

Platte was decommissioned June 30, 1999, and was turned over to the Maritime Administration November 29, 2001, when she joined the James River Reserve Fleet, Fort Eustis, Virginia.

Red Cloud YT-268
Named for Oglala Lakota Indian Chief born in what is now Nebraska.
(*Hiawatha* class harbor tug)

Displacement: 310 tons Length: 100' Width: 28' Draft: 10' Crew: 17

The *Red Cloud* was built by Birchfield Boiler, Inc., of Tacoma, Washington. She was launched May 2, 1942, and placed in service March 8, 1943. She was reclassified YTB (large harbor tug) May 15, 1944, and again to YTM (medium harbor tug) in February 1962. After service on the west coast during World War II, she remained active into 1974 as a harbor tug in the San Francisco Bay area.

USS *Reynolds* DE-91 & DE-42
Named for Blair, Nebraska native ENS Dudley Louis Reynolds, USN.
(*Evarts* class destroyer escort DE-42)

Displacement: 1,150 tons Length: 289' Width: 35' Draft: 11' Crew: 156

Dudley L. Reynolds was born at Blair, Nebraska November 20, 1910. He enlisted in the Navy January 4, 1928 and was Warranted Machinist February 18, 1938. He was commissioned Ensign July 23, 1942. After serving briefly on the *Saratoga*, he was assigned to the cruiser *Pensacola* CA-24. Ensign Reynolds was killed on the cruiser during the Battle of Tassafaronga, Solomon Islands November 30, 1942.

The first *Reynolds* DE-91 was slated for transfer to the Royal Navy before it was launched in October 1943.

The second *Reynolds* DE-42 was built by the Puget Sound Navy Yard, at Bremerton, Washington. The destroyer escort originally was intended to go to the Royal Navy but it was launched August 1, 1943, sponsored by Mrs. D. L. Reynolds (widow). She was commissioned in the U.S. Navy November 1, 1943, with Lieutenant Commander Edward P. Adams in command.

By January 27, 1944, *Reynolds* was screening *White Plains* CVE-66 to the Pacific Theatre. From February through May, she served under Commander, Submarine Training Force, then resuming escort duties with a voyage to Eniwetok. On July 28, 1944, she assisted *Wyman* DE-38 in the sinking of Japanese submarine *I-55*.

She was assigned to different task forces and continued front line Pacific operations through the end of the war. She was in Tokyo Bay in September and screened refueling operations.

The USS *Reynolds* was decommissioned December 5, 1945, at Mare Island Navy Yard. *Reynolds* was awarded eight battle stars for World War II service. She was sold and delivered to Mr. John L. Key of San Francisco April 28, 1947.

USS *Walter S. Brown* DE-258
Named for North Loup, Nebraska native Aircraft Machinist Mate 2nd Class
Walter S. Brown
(*Evarts* class destroyer escort)

Displacement: 1,150 tons Length: 289' Width: 35' Draft: 11' Crew: 156

Walter S. Brown was born in North Loup, Nebraska in March 1916. At 24, he enlisted in the Navy in January 1940. He was assigned to Patrol Squadron 24 at the Kaneohe Bay Naval Air Station, Hawaii, where he worked on Catalina seaplanes. On December 7, 1941, the base came under attack by Japanese aircraft. Petty Officer Brown was killed in the attack and was later commended by his commanding officer for his selfless bravery when he took action in defending the base.

The *Walter S. Brown* was built at the Boston Navy Yard during only six months of construction in 1943. She served in the Atlantic Fleet as a convoy escort. During May 1944 while escorting Convoy UGS-40 at the Straits of Gibraltar she came under attack by six enemy planes. The convoy commander later commended the *Walter S. Browns'* performance which he said in concert with the other escorts, broke up the enemy attack and prevented allied losses.

The USS *Walter S. Brown* was decommissioned in October 1945 and sold for scrap in 1948.

SS *Cornhusker State* ACS-6
Named for the state of Nebraska's nickname.
(*Gopher State* class auxiliary crane ship)

Displacement: 31,500 tons Length: 610' Width: 78' Draft: 33' Crew: unknown

The *SS Cornhusker State* was built by the Bath Iron Works Corporation, of Bath, Maine and launched November 2, 1968. It was delivered June 20, 1969.

Although not a commissioned vessel of the U. S. Navy, the ship is a member of the U.S. Maritime Administration's Ready Reserve Force (RRF), an active reserve of ships. The RRF ensures that the nation can maintain the surge capability needed to respond unilaterally to security threats in geographic areas not covered by NATO. The fleet assures quick-response-shipping with 76 vessels designed to meet special military requirements. The RRF has supported U.S. and allied operations in Somalia, Haiti, Bosnia, Croatia, Australia, South Korea and Central America.

During the fiscal year 2002, the auxiliary crane ship *Cornhusker State* was activated to participate in Operation Enduring Freedom (OEF). The ship, which served from November 5, 2001 to May 1, 2002, was the only RRF ship activated specifically to support OEF combat operations in Afghanistan. The *Cornhusker State* received the Maritime Administration's Professional Ship Award in November 2002. There are three ships in this class; *Gopher State* ACS-4; *Flickertail State* ACS-5; and *Cornhusker State* ACS-6.

Chapter 9

Omaha's Freedom Park Naval Museum

In 1971, the Hazard Corporation was formed when the World War II mine-sweeper USS *Hazard* AM-240 was purchased by Omaha businessmen. The corporation outbid the Mexican and Portuguese governments to acquire the *Hazard*. The ship was brought to Omaha via the Mississippi and Missouri Rivers and docked at Dodge Park. The corporation made a deal with the City of Omaha to lease property in what is now known as Freedom Park, along the Missouri River. This location tied in with riverfront development that continues to this day with the addition of the Quest Center convention complex. The Freedom Park organization bought the ship from the Hazard Corporation and began acquiring more naval items for display. The sale of pickle cards helped finance further purchases.

The Freedom Park Naval Museum is situated on 4.3 acres of land at 2497 Freedom Park Road, south of the Omaha airport and currently is operated by the Greater Omaha Military Historical Society, a nonprofit organization. The park is dedicated, "In honor of those who served, in tribute to those who perished, in gratitude of those now serving."

Still a highlight of the museum, the *Hazard* has been designated a National Historic Landmark. She is in remarkably complete condition and is one of the best preserved warships of World War II. It is amazing to see the anti-aircraft guns, the motor whaleboat and all the electronic gear, including the dishes, still on board!

The *Admirable* class minesweeper displaces 540 tons, is 184' long, 33' wide and has a 10' draft, with a crew complement of 104. It is armed with one, three-inch, two 40mm, and six 20mm guns (and depth charges when in service). She was built by the Winslow Marine Railway & Shipbuilding Company, of Winslow, Washington. This class was slightly reduced in size compared with previous minesweepers to accommodate the numerical need for them during wartime. They were first classed as coastal minesweepers (AM c), but were appropriately reclassified as minesweepers (AM) prior to the start of construction. The Winslow Company built several of the 180 strong *Admirable* class. In 1945, 34 of these ships were given to the Soviet navy.[1] Launched on May 21, 1944, with Miss Joanne R. Heddens as sponsor, she was commissioned on October 31, 1944, with Lieutenant Curtis B. Tibbals, USNR, in command.

The minesweepers were known as the first ships to arrive in enemy waters and the last to leave. Their work was essential for the success of U.S. Naval operations even though the American public knows little about them.

She departed San Francisco on January 5, 1945, screening a convoy to Pearl Harbor. *Hazard* then escorted convoys between Pearl and Eniwetok, and then to Ulithi Atoll and Kossol Roads before reaching Leyte for supplies.

In March, she worked with Admiral Killand's Western Islands Attack Group in support of the invasion of Okinawa during March–June. During this time, she participated in anti-submarine patrol and clearing mine fields around Kerama Retto. The ship went on to minesweeping missions in the East China Sea.

After the Japanese surrendered, the *Hazard* performed sweeping operations in the Yellow Sea and Jinsen, Korea, searching for occupation forces. Through the end of October, she cleared the Sasebo, Japan area for mines. Arriving at San Diego on December 19, she headed to Galveston, Texas via the Panama Canal on January 31, 1946.

The USS *Hazard* was decommissioned at Galveston on July 27, 1946 and joined the Reserve Fleet. *Hazard* was awarded three battle stars for WWII service. On February 7, 1955, she was reclassified MSF-240 (minesweeper-fleet), and remained in the Texas Group, Atlantic Reserve Fleet until finally sold as surplus.

The USS *Marlin* SST-2 is another important member of the "Freedom Park Navy". The training submarine (*T-1* class), displaces 303 tons, is 131 feet long, 14 feet wide, has a 12-foot draft and a crew of 14. It was armed with two torpedo tubes.

Marlin was built by the Electric Boat Division of the General Dynamics Corporation in Groton, Connecticut. She was launched on October 14, 1953, and sponsored by Mrs. William R. DeLoach. It was commissioned as *T-2* on November 20, 1953, with Lieutenant Edward Holt, USN, in command.

She got underway from New London, CT in January 1954, and headed to her home port, Key West, Florida. *T-2* was assigned to Submarine Squadron 12, Submarine Force, Atlantic Fleet, and operated between Florida and Guantanamo

Bay, Cuba. She performed as a target and training ship and helped to evaluate submarine and anti-submarine equipment and tactics for the Fleet Sonar School at Key West. She participated in fleet operations with *T-1* (*Mackerel*), *Amberjack* SS-522, *Batfish* SS-310, and *Chivo* SS-341, along with Commander, Mine Force, for mine warfare maneuvers.

On May 15, 1956, she was renamed *Marlin*, and continued to operate into the late 1960s, in the Key West region as a target and training submarine.

Freedom Park also offers visitors several anchors and propellers to inspect including a mammoth 30,000 pound anchor from the USS *Wasp* CV-18 (aircraft carrier). A U.S. Navy A-4 Skyhawk, A-7 Corsair and a Coast Guard HH-52A helicopter form part of the Park's "air wing." Weapons on display include a 5-inch gun turret, a 1.1-inch anti-aircraft gun and an ASROC missile launcher. Visitors enter through the office and gift shop that also includes equipment, uniforms and photos from the USS *Omaha* (submarine and light cruiser) as well as the USS *Nebraska* SSBN-739.

The Freedom Park Naval Museum provides naval buffs and anyone interested in history, a place to enjoy right in the heart of the America.

Omaha's Freedom Park Naval Museum is home to the WWII
minesweeper USS Hazard (AM-240) and the USS Marlin (SST-2).
(Author's photo)

POSTSCRIPT

We waited patiently while final docking procedures were completed. I studied each sailor as he left the ship. Like the sailors of the battleship *Nebraska*, they looked forward to good chow and coming home.

Navy officials spoke, welcoming the crew of the submarine to their new home-port on the West Coast. Our group, from the state of Nebraska, was recognized for our attendance and continued support of the ship and crews.

After we crossed over the brow and set foot on the black deck, we were ushered to the aft hatch. As we walked, we noticed faint outlines and a series of numbers, 21, 22, 23, 24, under our feet, which were the Trident missile doors. It was comforting to know that *Nebraska* and others like her sail to protect us, but the hope that those doors never need to be opened in wartime, is the most comforting. The most important function of the missile submarine is deterrence. Errant foreign powers surely realize that if they were to launch a nuclear weapon at the United States, they would never know if their attack was successful.

We carefully climbed down a long ladder that took us inside a world of steel, machinery and electronics. In fact, it was amazing to see the amount of equipment that was packed inside. While not cramped like a WWII *Gato* sub, there didn't appear to be an overabundance of room. The "Cornhusker Café" (crew's mess) seemed to be the largest space which featured a serving line at one end and rows of tables throughout. The sailors on duty we visited with looked so young, but their mere presence as part of the crew affirmed their highly technical skill level. Being assigned to a submarine requires a high degree of education and training in their respective fields. As part of that training, every member of the crew, no matter his specialty, has to learn and be certified on *every* system on the ship thus earning his "dolphins." The dolphin badge was suggested by Captain Ernest J. King (later Fleet Admiral) in 1923, for the purpose of distinguishing "qualified" submariners.[1] All of the sailors we observed were proudly wearing their dolphins. Additionally, all members of the crew are required to perform duties outside of their specialty fields.

While touring the sub, I silently wondered what the crewmembers of the old battleship *Nebraska* would have thought of this vessel. I imagine the first thing they would have liked about it was not having to coal her. The comfortable below decks climate, no matter where on the globe they were, surely would have found favor. They might have missed their port calls however, as missile submarines don't visit foreign ports like other naval ships. I'm betting the positives would have far outweighed the negatives.

As we climbed back up that same ladder, we were quite aware of the great privilege afforded us in touring the *Nebraska*. Submarines are a highly secretive part of our Navy, as well they should be. The submarine's crew does share a common heritage with all the sailors who have come before them who have served on a ship named *Nebraska,* and they are all part of the proud history of the United States Navy.

*"The Navy has both a tradition and a future—and we look with
pride and confidence in both directions."*

—Admiral George Anderson, Chief of Naval Operations
August 1, 1961

ABOUT THE AUTHOR

The author is a retired lieutenant with the Hastings, Nebraska Police Department. He graduated from the 174th Session of the FBI National Academy at Quantico, Virginia in 1993.

Mr. McCord's published works include the books; *Police Cars—A Photographic History* (1991), *Cars of the State Police & Highway Patrol* (1994), *Law Enforcement Memorabilia* (1999), and *Hastings—The Queen City of the Plains* (2001).

In 1997, he appeared on the History Channel in "Police Cars", part of their "Wheels of Survival" program.

McCord researches police and naval history including the historic position of naval "Master at Arms".

He currently serves as president of the Friend's of the Hastings Public Library Board, is a member of the Adams County Historical Society Board of Directors and is a member of the Nebraska Writer's Guild, Big Red Sub Club, Nebraska Admirals Association (2005) and the Police Officer's Association of Nebraska.

McCord continues the historical research of the USS *Nebraskas* and is interested in documents, photographs and items relating to them.

APPENDIX A:

OHIO CLASS SUBMARINES & COMMISSION DATES

OHIO CLASS MISSILE SUBMARINES
AND COMMISSION DATES

*OHIO**	SSBN-726	1981
*MICHIGAN**	SSBN-727	1982
*FLORIDA**	*SSBN-728*	*1983*
*GEORGIA**	SSBN-729	1984
HENRY M. JACKSON	SSBN-730	1984
ALABAMA	SSBN-731	1985
ALASKA	SSBN-732	1986
NEVADA	SSBN-733	1986
TENNESSEE	SSBN-734	1988
PENNSYLVANIA	SSBN-735	1989
WEST VIRGINIA	SSBN-736	1990
KENTUCKY	SSBN-737	1991
MARYLAND	SSBN-738	1992
NEBRASKA	SSBN-739	1993
RHODE ISLAND	SSBN-740	1994
MAINE	SSBN-741	1995
WYOMING	SSBN-742	1996
LOUISIANA	SSBN-743	1997

*Re-designated as SSGN (Guided Missile Submarine) in 2004.

APPENDIX B:

OF INTEREST

Big Red Sub Club
c/o Jerry Swift
3664 Huntington Ave.
Omaha, NE 68112-2944
www.bigredsubclub.com

Nebraska Admirals Association
P.O. Box 83723
Lincoln, NE 68501
www.nebraskaadmirals.org

Nebraska Submarine Veterans
(United States Submarine Veterans)
www.ussv-centralregion.org

Freedom Park Naval Museum
2497 Freedom Park Road
Omaha, NE 68110

Dept. of the Navy—Naval Historical Center
805 Kidder Breese SE, Washington Navy Yard
Washington, D.C. 20374-5060
www.history.navy.mil

Submarine Force Museum
Naval Submarine Base New London
Groton, CT 06349-5571
(Home of the first nuclear submarine, USS *Nautilus*)
www.ussnautilus.org

Naval Historical Foundation
1306 Dahlgren Ave. SE, Washington Navy Yard
Washington, D.C. 20374-5055
www.navyhistory.org

General Dynamics-Electric Boat Division
75 Eastern Point Rd.
Groton, CT 06340-4989
www.gdeb.com

Undersea Warfare
Official U.S. Submarine Force magazine
www.chinfo.navy.mil
Available from:
Supt. of Documents, GPO
P.O. Box 371954
Pittsburgh, PA 15250-7954

Seapower
Magazine of the Navy League
Navy League of the United States
"Citizens in support of the sea services"
2300 Wilson Blvd.
Arlington, VA 22201-3308

Sea Classics
Challenge Publications Inc.
Subscription Offices
P.O. Box 16149
North Hollywood, CA 91615
www.challengeweb.com

Historic Naval Ships Association
c/o *Albacore* Park
600 Market Street
Portsmouth, NH 03801-3361
www.hnsa.org
The Historic Naval Ships Association offers, through Challenge Publications (9509 Vassar Ave. Unit A, Chatsworth, CA 91311), the *Historic Naval Ships Guide*, which is a guide to naval ship museums across the U.S.(including Omaha, NE) and around the world. Highly recommended.

Naval History
U.S. Naval Institute
2062 Generals Hwy.
Annapolis, MD 21401
www.navalinstitute.org

Naval Institute Press (Book publishing arm of U.S. Naval Institute)
www.usni.org/press

U.S. Navy Memorial Foundation
www.lonesailor.org

All Hands
Magazine of the U.S. Navy
2713 Mitscher Rd. SW
Anacostia Annex, D.C. 20373-5819
www.news.navy.mil/allhands.asp

NOTES

CHAPTER 1. THE FIRST *NEBRASKA* AND THE PRE-1900 NAVY

1. Beach, *United States Navy*, 47.
2. Ibid., 57–58.
3. Ibid., 66–67.
4. Spears, *A History*, 156.
5. Ibid., 160.
6. The USS *Choctaw (Nebraska)* was sold March 28, 1866 at New Orleans.
7. Silverstone, *Civil War Navies*, 9.
8. Beach, *United States Navy*, 342.

CHAPTER 2. MORAN BROTHERS BUILD THE BATTLESHIP *NEBRASKA*

1. Peacock, *Rosario Yesterdays*, 11.
2. Hanson, "The USS *Nebraska*", 107.
3. Photograph of Mary Nain Mickey at Seattle. Nebraska State Historical Society photo archives.
4. Reilly, Scheina, *American Battleships*, 144.
5. Coontz, *Mississippi to the Sea*, 275.
6. Potter, "The Silver Service for the USS *Nebraska*", 117.
7. Peacock, *Rosario Yesterdays*, 66–67.

CHAPTER 3. MEMBER OF TEDDY'S GREAT WHITE FLEET

1. "Professor Fling Urges a Larger American Navy," *Hastings Daily Tribune*, Oct. 22, 1908.
2. Carter, *Incredible Great White Fleet*, 11.
3. Reckner, *Roosevelt's Great White Fleet*, 29–30.
4. Reilly, Scheina, *American Battleships*, 7, 244.

5. Navy Department, *Information Relative to the Voyage of the United States Atlantic Fleet Around the World Dec. 16, 1907–Feb. 22, 1909* (Washington, D.C.: Government Printing Office, 1910), 22–23.
6. Carter, *Incredible Great White Fleet*, 26.
7. Schroeder, *Naval Service*, 313.
8. Dates in Naval History, August, Department of the Navy, Naval Historical Center.
9. Naval Cover commemorating the establishment of the first post office on board American Naval vessel. Author's collection.
10. Young, John P., "Navophilately Before the USCS, 1930–32," *Universal Ship Cancellation Society*, 1992, 1.
11. Reckner, *Roosevelt's Great White Fleet*, 87–88.
12. Coontz, *True Anecdotes*, 115–116.
13. Coontz, *Mississippi to the Sea*, 288.
14. Carter, *Incredible Great White Fleet*, 140.
15. Coontz, *True Anecdotes*, 41–42.
16. Coontz, *Mississippi to the Sea*, 292.
17. Reckner, *Roosevelt's Great White Fleet*, 151.
18. Coontz, *Mississippi to the Sea*, 294.
19. Wimmel, *Theodore Roosevelt and the Great White Fleet*, 242.
20. Carter, *Incredible Great White Fleet*, 173.

CHAPTER 4. WAR SERVICE & FINAL HARBOR

1. Friedman, *U.S. Battleships*, 83.
2. *Dictionary of American Naval Fighting Ships*, s.v. *Nebraska*.
3. Friedman, *U.S. Battleships*, 170.
4. Reilly, Scheina, *American Battleships*, 12, 244.
5. *Dictionary of American Battleships*, s.v. *Nebraska*.
6. Peacock, *Rosario Yesterdays*, 36.
7. John P. Ridgway to Mrs. R. L. Cochran, Feb. 15, 1936, Omaha, Nebraska.
8. "Conserving Part of Nebraska's Heritage," *Regional Alliance for Preservation*, (Fall 1999).
9. "New Troopship to be Named After Coontz," *Hannibal Courier*, Apr. 20, 1944.
10. *Dictionary of American Naval Fighting Ships*, s.v. *Coontz*.
11. Hurly, Hagood, Thomson, *Hannibal Heritage*, 82–84.
12. "Ship Made a Splash a Century Ago," *Seattle Times*, Oct. 2, 2004.

CHAPTER 5. DIVING-BOATS TO BOOMERS

1. Hutchinson, *Submarines*, 9.
2. Goodspeed, *U.S. Navy*, 220–221.
3. Rodengen, *Legend of Electric Boat*, 18–19.
4. Hutchinson, *Submarines*, 186.

CHAPTER 6. "BIG RED"—DEFENDER OF PEACE

1. Clinton Orr, letter to author, Nov. 12, 2004.
2. "Departing, *Nebraska* to Leave in 2004," *The Periscope*, Oct. 22, 2003.

CHAPTER 7. "BIG RED" PRIDE RUNS DEEP

1. Website, *Nebraska Admiral's Association*.
2. Commissioning address, July, 10, 1993, J. James Exon Papers, Exon Library, Lincoln, Nebraska.

CHAPTER 8. NEBRASKA NAME RELATED SHIPS

1. "Man Who Sailed On USS *Grand Island* Thanks Ship's Namesake," *Grand Island Independent*, Aug. 15, 1999.
2. *Memoirs of Thomas O. Selfridge, Jr.* (New York: G.P. Putnam's Sons, 1924), 246.

CHAPTER 9. OMAHA'S FREEDOM PARK NAVAL MUSEUM

1. Lenton, *American Gunboats*, 46–47.

POSTSCRIPT

1. Kaplan, *Run Silent*, 80.

BIBLIOGRAPHY

BOOKS

Beach, Edward L. *The United States Navy A 200-Year History*. New York: Houghton Mifflin Co., 1986.

Carter, Samuel. *The Incredible Great White Fleet*. New York: Macmillan & Co., 1971.

Coontz, Robert E. *From the Mississippi to the Sea*. Philadelphia: Dorrance, 1930.

————. *True Anecdotes of an Admiral*. Philadelphia: Dorrance, 1935.

Friedman, Norman. *U.S. Battleships—An Illustrated Design History*. Annapolis: Naval Institute, Press, 1985.

Goodspeed, M. Hill. *U.S. Navy The Complete History*. Washington: Naval Historical Foundation, 2003.

Hagood, J. Hurley & Roberta, and Thomson, Dave. *Hannibal Heritage*. Marceline: Heritage House Publishing, 2003.

Hall, Richard Compton. *Submarine Warfare Monsters & Midgets*. Poole, U.K.: Blandford Press, 1985.

Harris, LTCDR Brayton. *The Age of the Battleship 1890–1922*. New York: Franklin Watts, 1965.

Hutchinson, Robert. *Submarines War Beneath the Waves From 1776 to the Present Day*. New York: Harper Collins, 2001.

Kaplan, Philip. *Run Silent*. London, U.K.: Aurum Press, 2002.

Kaufman, Steve & Yogi. *Silent Chase—Submarines of the U.S. Navy*. Charlottesville: Thomasson Grant, Inc., 1989.

Konstam, Angus. *Union Monitor 1861–65*. Botley, U.K.: Osprey Pub. Ltd., 2002.

————. *Union River Ironclad 1861–65*. Botley, U.K.: Osprey Pub. Ltd., 2002.

Lenton, H. T. *American Gunboats and Minesweepers*. London, U.K.: MacDonald & Jane's, 1974.

Mack, William P. & Connell, Royal W. *Naval Ceremonies, Customs and Traditions*. Annapolis: 5th Ed. Naval Institute Press, 1981.

Newhart, Max R. *American Battleships—A Pictorial History of BB-1 to BB-71.* Missoula: Pictorial Histories Publishing Co., 2003.

Peacock, Christopher M. *Rosario Yesterdays A Pictorial History.* Eastsound: Rosario Productions, 1985.

Preston, Antony. *Battleships of WW1—An Illustrated Encyclopedia of the Battleships of All Nations 1914–1918.* New York: Galahad Books 1972.

———. *Submarines.* Greenwich: Bison Books, 1982.

Reckner, James R. *Teddy Roosevelt's Great White Fleet.* Annapolis: Naval Institute Press, 1988.

Reilly, John C. Jr. & Scheina, Robert L. *American Battleships 1886–1923.* Annapolis: Naval Institute Press, 1980.

Rodengen, Jeffrey L. *The Legend of Electric Boat.* Fort Lauderdale: Write Stuff Syndicate, 1994.

Schroeder, Seaton. *A Half Century of Naval Service.* New York: D. Appleton & Co., 1922.

Selfridge, Thomas O. Jr. *Memoirs of Thomas O. Selfridge, Jr.* New York: G. P. Putnam's Sons, 1924

Silverstone, Paul H. *Civil War Navies 1855–1883.* Annapolis: Naval Institute Press, 2001.

———. *The Sailing Navy 1775–1854.* Annapolis: Naval Institute Press, 2001.

Spears, John R. *A History of the United States Navy.* New York: Charles Scribner's Sons, 1908.

Waller, Douglas C. *Big Red—Three Months on Board a Trident Nuclear Submarine.* New York: Harper Collins Pub. Inc., 2001.

Wimmel, Kenneth. *Theodore Roosevelt and the Great White Fleet.* Dulles: Brassey's, 2000.

GOVERNMENT DOCUMENTS

U.S. Department of the Navy. Official Records of the Union and Confederate Navies in the War of the Rebellion. Published under the direction of the Secretary of the Navy by C. C. Marsh, CAPT USN (Ret)—Series I, Volume 20, 21, 22, 23, 24, 25, 27. Series II, Volume 1. Washington: GPO, 1905–1921.

U.S. Department of the Navy. Commander in Chief, U.S., Atlantic Fleet. *List of Vessels and Roster of Officers of the Vessels of the United States Atlantic Fleet Making the Cruise to the Pacific Coast.* Washington: GPO, 1907.

U.S. Department of the Navy. Bureau of Navigation. *Men on Board Ships of the Atlantic Fleet Bound for the Pacific Dec. 16, 1907, with Home Addresses in the United States Arranged Alphabetically by States, Cities, and Towns of the U.S.* Washington: GPO, 1908.

U.S. Department of the Navy. *Information Relative to the Voyage of the United States Atlantic Fleet Around the World, Dec. 16, 1907–Feb. 22, 1909.* Washington: GPO, 1910.

U.S. Department of the Navy. Naval History Division. *Ships of the United States Navy, Christening, Launching, and Commissioning* 2nd. Ed. Prepared by John C. Reilly, Jr. Washington: GPO, 1975.

ARTICLES

"Conditions of the Battleships After the Long Cruise." *Scientific American* 100:386 (May 22, 1909).

Daly, Frederick T. "Nebraska-Related Names of United States Navy Ships." *Nebraska History* (Nebraska State Historical Society), 69, no. 3 (Summer/Fall 1995).

Hanson, James A. "The USS Nebraska." *Nebraska History* (Nebraska State Historical Society), 76, nos. 2 & 3 (Fall 1988).

"How Warships are Scrapped." *Literary Digest* 74:20–1 (Aug. 12, 1922).

Muschamp, E. A. "Honorably Discharged." *Collier's* 70:12 J1 15 1922.

"Our First Line of Defense, A Battleship Division in Maneuvers." *Scientific American* (Oct. 19, 1912).

Paradise, Judith Ann. "Robert E. Coontz, Admiral from Hannibal." *Nemoscope* (Northeast Missouri State Teachers College), 13, no.3 (Spring 1959).

Potter, Gail DeBuse. "The Silver Service for the USS Nebraska." *Nebraska History* (Nebraska State Historical Society), 69, no.3 (Fall 1988).

"Recently Completed Battleship."*(Nebraska) Scientific American* 95:77, 82 (Aug. 4, 1906).

Schierbrand, W. von. "Robert Moran, Builder of the Nebraska." *World To—Day* 9:1328–30 (Dec. 1905).

Thompson, Pamela S. "Around the Horn." *L Lincoln's Premiere Lifestyle Magazine* (Lincoln, Nebraska) 3 (Dec. 2004).

Walker, J. B. "Scrapping the Battleships." *Scientific American* 126:185–8 (Mar. 1922).

"Washington Conference Battleship." *Scientific American* 128:304 (May 1923).

NEWSPAPERS

Grand Island (Nebraska) *Independent*
Hannibal (Missouri) *Courier-Post*
Hastings (Nebraska) *Daily Republican*
Hastings (Nebraska) *Daily Tribune*
Kings Bay (Georgia) *Periscope*
Kitsap (Washington) *Sun*
New York (New York) *Herald*
Omaha (Nebraska) *Daily Bee*
Omaha (Nebraska) *Daily News*
Omaha (Nebraska) *World Herald*
Seattle (Washington) *Post-Intelligencer*
Seattle (Washington) *Times*
Wymore (Nebraska) *Arbor State*

LETTERS, MISC

Moran Bros. Co., Launching Program for U.S. Battleship *Nebraska*, Oct. 7, 1904. Nebraska State Historical Society Archives, Lincoln, Nebraska.

Winthrop, Beekman, Acting Secretary of the Navy. Letter to Congressman M. P. Kincaid, July 9, 1909. Nebraska State Historical Society Archives, Lincoln, Nebraska.

Winthrop, Beekman, Acting Secretary of the Navy. Letter to Clarence S. Paine, Sec. Nebraska State Historical Society, Oct. 23, 1909. Nebraska State Historical Society Archives, Lincoln, Nebraska.

Winthrop, Beekman, Acting Secretary of the Navy. Letter to C. S. Paine, Sec. Nebraska State Historical Society, Nov. 4, 1909. Nebraska State Historical Society Archives, Lincoln, Nebraska.

Swanson, Claude, Secretary of the Navy. Letter to Gov. Roy L. Cochran, Feb. 3, 1936. Nebraska State Historical Society Archives, Lincoln, Nebraska.

United States Government Bill of Lading for return of silver service, Feb. 3, 1936. Nebraska State Historical Society Archives, Lincoln, Nebraska.

Ridgway, John P. Letter to Mrs. R. L. Cochran, Feb. 15, 1936. Nebraska State Historical Society Archives, Lincoln, Nebraska.

Smith & Co. Ltd. Description of Silver Service (USS *Nebraska*), 1936. Nebraska State Historical Society Archives, Lincoln, Nebraska.

Smith, A. Franklin of Smith & Co. Ltd. Letter To Mrs. Roy Cochran May 7, 1936. Nebraska State Historical Society Archives, Lincoln, Nebraska.

Cochran, Roy, Governor of Nebraska. Letter to Claude S. Swanson, Secretary Of the Navy, April 14, 1936. Nebraska State Historical Society Archives, Lincoln, Nebraska.

Paine, Clarence S. Report of the Secretary, Nebraska State Historical Society 1909. Nebraska State Historical Society Archives, Lincoln, Nebraska.

Nebraska Admirals Association. Newsletters, *Echoes from Sonar*, May 1991, November, 1992, March 1993, September 1993. Author's collection.

Nebraska Admirals Association. Society of Nebraska Admirals Bylaws, April, 4, 1987. Author's collection.

The Big Red Sub Club News 6 nos. 2–3, 7 no.1. Big Red Sub Club. Author's collection.

Exon, J. James. USS *Nebraska* Commissioning Address, July 10, 1993. Exon Library, Lincoln, Nebraska.

"Conserving Part of Nebraska's Heritage." *Regional Alliance for Preservation* Fall 1999. Author's collection.

INDEX

(Nebraska related naval ships in **bold** face.)

978-0-595-36655-2
0-595-36655-4

Printed in the United Kingdom
by Lightning Source UK Ltd.
108401UKS00001B/105